CHARLES G. FINNEY'S DOCTRINE OF THE
BAPTISM OF THE HOLY SPIRIT

CHARLES G. FINNEY'S DOCTRINE OF THE BAPTISM OF THE HOLY SPIRIT

John Leroy Gresham, Jr.

HENDRICKSON
PUBLISHERS
PEABODY, MASSACHUSETTS 01961-3473

Many of Finney's writings referred to in this book are now
in print in the Finney series
edited by Louis G. Parkhurst and
published by Bethany Fellowship
Press.

Second printing – January, 1989

Copyright © 1987
Hendrickson Publishers, Inc.
P.O. Box 3473
Peabody, MA 01961–3473
Printed in the United States of America

ISBN 0–913573–47–7

TABLE OF CONTENTS

ACKNOWLEDGEMENTS

I am indebted to Dr. Timothy Smith whose research on Finney's Doctrine of Spirit Baptism provided the foundation upon which this present work builds. I also wish to express my appreciation to Dr. Stephen Franklin who read this study in its original form as a Master's thesis at Wheaton College Graduate School and encouraged me to seek its publication. Many thanks as well to my wife and parents for their encouragement and support in all my academic endeavors. Finally, thanks to Patrick Alexander for his helpful editing.

INTRODUCTION

IN HIS *Religious History of the American People*, Sidney E. Ahlstrom wrote, "Finney is an immensely important man in American history by any standard of measure."[1] A former president of Wheaton College, V. Raymond Edman, referred to Finney as the "pre-eminent American Revivalist."[2] Another historian wrote that Finney was "of epoch-making significance in the history of evangelism."[3] Still another claims that it was Charles G. Finney, "perhaps more than any other single individual," who has had "the greatest impact upon the formation of American Evangelical Christianity and the eventual development of the American Pentecostal Phenomenon."[4]

In describing his impact upon Evangelicalism, most historians have stressed Finney's emphasis on human ability and responsibility. Finney played a tremendous role in the "Arminianizing" of American Evangelicalism, if not always in its belief, at least in its practices. His "new measures" of promoting revivals became widely accepted. His controversial use of the "anxious seat" gained wide acceptance among Evangelicals, in a modified form, as the evangelistic altar call. Professional evangelists who hold protracted mass meetings to promote "decisions for Christ" are walking in the footsteps of Finney.

Finney's greatest impact upon American Christianity, however, is probably not his emphasis upon human ability, but his equal emphasis, seldom noted, upon the individual's dependence on the Holy Spirit in salvation, sanctification, and service. Within Finney's overall theology, his understanding of the Baptism in the Holy Spirit has generated the greatest impact upon Evangelicalism and beyond. Only recently has the impact of this aspect of Finney's thought been noted. Timothy Smith, for one, has pointed to Finney's important role in the development of the Holiness doctrine of the Baptism in the Holy Spirit, as well as his role in the "Higher Life" or "Keswick" movement.[5] Finney's significance in the development of Pentecostalism has been noted by F. D. Bruner.[6] The purpose of this study is to describe this influential aspect of Finney's theology—the Baptism in the Holy Spirit.

Some previous studies have paved the way for an understanding of Finney's doctrine of the Baptism in the Spirit, but are in themselves incomplete. Timothy Smith's study, while very helpful, focuses on Finney's understanding of Spirit Baptism only in relation to sanctification and is based entirely on one series of articles written by Finney in 1839–1840.[7] Obviously there are many other writings in which Finney discussed his view. Moreover, in many of these, the focus is not upon sanctification, but rather on the Baptism in the Spirit as an enduement of power for ministry. James Cafone's study of Finney's pneumatology is also a quite useful introduction and survey of Finney's understanding of the work of the Spirit.[8] That study, however, having a broader scope, devotes only a short section to the Baptism in the Spirit. Finney himself, furthermore, did not devote a section of his *Systematic Theology* specifically to this subject. Therefore, there is a need for a description and interpretation of the various articles, sermons, and tracts in which Finney did discuss the Baptism in the Spirit. That is the goal of this present study.

"Baptism in the Holy Spirit" in this study refers to a post-regeneration spiritual experience. In Finney's theology, regeneration and conversion are different terms for the same experience—the beginning of the Christian life. Very early in his ministry Finney emphasized the need for a subsequent work or experience of the Spirit, an experience he eventually came to call "the Baptism of the Holy Spirit." This experience completed the work of sanctification begun in regeneration by giving a new constancy and permanency to the Christian's consecration. According to Finney, regeneration implied total consecration, which he considered, in one sense, to be entire sanctification. It was not "entire" or "complete" only in the sense that it was not unceasing or permanent. The Christian needed the Baptism in the Holy Spirit to establish him in a life of unceasing, permanent consecration to God. In that sense, Finney viewed this experience as the means to "entire sanctification." Finney also saw the Baptism in the Spirit as a divine empowering for ministry. Through this experience the Christian received a divine anointing which empowered his preaching and his praying, and brought greater effectiveness in winning souls to Christ. Both the permanent sanctification and the empowered preaching and prayer resulted from the experiential union with Christ as He was revealed by the Holy Spirit. The Baptism in the Spirit was that experience which introduced the believer into this experience of living union with Christ. Spirit Baptism was not a one-time, unrepeatable experience from Finney's perspective, but was instead to be experienced again and again, bringing the believer into new heights of spiritual life and service.

This study will begin by providing a general introduction to Finney's life, his theology, and the theological, historical, and cultural influences upon his thought. This will be followed by a survey of his important writings on the Baptism in the Holy Spirit. Recognizing that Finney's ideas were essentially the products of his own profound spiritual experiences, we will also examine his descriptions of his own Spirit Baptisms. This chronological survey of Finney's thought and experience will provide a general introduction to that which follows.

From there I will take a topical approach. First, I will review Finney's understanding of Spirit Baptism as the means to entire and permanent sanctification and seek to understand Finney in light of his theology of Christian perfection and his analysis of the process of sanctification. Then, I will take a closer look at those writings in which Finney presented the Baptism in the Spirit as the "enduement of power from on high," power not only for preaching but also for prayer. I will show that Finney's understanding of the Baptism in the Spirit as experiential union with Christ underlies both the emphasis on sanctification and on power.

Following that, I will discuss two aspects of Finney's view greatly criticized today: the idea of the Baptism in the Spirit as subsequent to regeneration and the related idea of "conditions" for receiving this baptism. With each of these, I will look at Finney's view in light of recent discussions and allow him to enter the current debate.

This will be followed by a comparison and interaction with subsequent views of the Baptism in the Spirit and an investigation of Finney's role in their development. I will then conclude with a summary and state what I believe to be the contributions Finney can offer to a contemporary understanding of the Baptism in the Spirit.

My goals for this study are first, to provide students of American church history and those interested in the historical roots of the Pentecostal and Holiness movements a clear and more thorough description of Finney's understanding of the Baptism in the Spirit than is now available; and second, for my fellow participants in the Charismatic movement, to share Finney's insights into this experience to aid in their own theological understanding of the Baptism in the Spirit.

FINNEY'S LIFE AND THEOLOGY:
A GENERAL INTRODUCTION

CHARLES G. FINNEY WAS BORN in Connecticut in 1792, but was
raised in western New York, which at that time was still
considered a frontier region. As a young man, he taught school briefly
and then began to study law. At the time of his conversion in 1821,
at the age of twenty-nine, he was an aspiring young lawyer in Adams,
New York. Following his dramatic conversion experience, Finney
claimed that he had "a retainer from the Lord Jesus Christ to plead
his cause" and left the law profession for the ministry.[1] Following two
years of study under his pastor, Finney received his license to preach,
and later, ordination in the Presbyterian Church. During this time,
Finney found little he could agree with in his pastor's theology and
gradually developed his own views through his independent study
of the Scriptures.

In 1824 Finney began itinerant preaching in the small villages of
western New York, later moving to the larger towns. By 1827 his highly
successful but controversial, direct, and forceful revival preaching had
brought him to national prominence. That same year Finney and
several of his supporters from western New York met with a group
of critics from the east in New Lebanon, New York. The results of
the New Lebanon Convention, as it was called, were inconclusive.
Ironically, the leader of the opposition, Lyman Beecher, would later
invite Finney to preach in his own church. In the years 1829–1832,
Finney preached in such large cities as Philadelphia, New York, and
Boston. The most successful revival of Finney's career occurred during
this period in Rochester, New York. Of this revival Finney wrote,

> The greatness of the work at Rochester at that time, attracted so much
> of the attention of ministers and Christians throughout the state of New
> York, throughout New England, and in many parts of the U.S., that the
> very fame of it was an efficient instrument in the hands of the Spirit
> of God in promoting the greatest revival of religion throughout the
> land that this country had then ever witnessed.[2]

In 1832 Finney became pastor of a new Presbyterian church in New York City, housed in a former theatre. It was in New York that Finney preached a series of sermons on revivals, which were printed in the *New York Evangelist* and later published as his *Lectures on Revivals of Religion*, Finney's most popular and influential book. Another important work, *Lectures to Professing Christians*, also originated in New York.

In 1835 Finney left the Presbyterian Church to become a Congregationalist. These denominations were closely united by the Plan of Union of 1801, but by this time the union was falling apart. Finney was never adamantly loyal to the doctrines of either Presbyterianism or Congregationalism, claiming to be "absolutely ashamed" of the Westminster Confession, the doctrinal basis of both denominations.[3]

The year 1835 also marked the beginning of Finney's involvement with Oberlin College, the new training school for revivalists and reformers in Ohio. In addition to his teaching duties as a professor of theology, Finney served as president of the school (1851–1866) and as pastor of the Oberlin Congregational Church (1837–1872). It was at Oberlin that Finney wrote and published his *Systematic Theology*. Many of his sermons and articles appeared in the *Oberlin Evangelist* and the *Oberlin Quarterly Review*.

During his time at Oberlin, Finney continued to make evangelistic tours, including two trips to England. After 1860, because of his health, he remained at Oberlin, where in 1868 he wrote his memoirs, though they were not published until after his death. He died in 1875, at almost 83 years of age.[4]

Thus while most prominent as an evangelist, Finney also served as a pastor, theological professor, and college president. His theology developed out of a profound religious experience and in a life of practical service in these varied roles. His thought also developed within a particular historical and religious milieu, the understanding of which is crucial for comprehending his theology.

THE CONTEXT OF FINNEY'S THEOLOGY

Finney's early ministry nearly coincided with the presidency of Andrew Jackson (1829–1837), and his theology reflected the "rugged individualism and the idea of progress" characteristic of the Jacksonian era.[5] The emphasis of Finney's theology upon humanity's ability and responsibility reflected the political discussions of the day concerning the common person's ability to govern himself. As with Jackson's democratic political views, so Finney's religious views expressed the individualism, freedom, self-reliance, and optimism experienced in the American western frontiers.[6]

Along with the feeling of freedom produced by the American experiences of frontier life and democratic self-government came the concern over control. Politicians and preachers were concerned that the freedom of the frontier and of democracy not turn into lawlessness and anarchy.[7] Thus, for many, including Finney, religion came to be seen as the necessary means of social control if the American experiment were to succeed. His theology, then, reflected both the freedom of the American experience and the concern to control that freedom. Thus, for Finney, revivals were not only a means of saving souls but of transforming individuals and, ultimately, society. Through revivalism, the church would usher in the millennial kingdom to America and the world. Finney believed that regeneration resulted in radical moral transformation and that Christians should be actively involved in reforming all areas of their society. Many of Finney's converts became active in temperance, anti-slavery, and other movements of the day.[8]

Finney's theology reflected not only the "Age of Jackson," but also an age referred to as "The Second Great Awakening." While Finney was a major contributor to this "Awakening," this general religious revival was larger than Finney himself. The beginning of this awakening preceded his own ministry, beginning in the late 1790s and early 1800s. There were prominent evangelists, most notably Asahel Nettleton (1783–1844), one of Finney's critics at the New Lebanon Convention, who were decidedly Calvinistic in their theology, and yet, very much successful revivalists. This was also a time of great revival and growth among the Methodists, Baptists, and other denominations besides those in which Finney regularly labored. The optimistic view of the perfectibility of humanity and society that Finney espoused was definitely influenced by the dramatic success religious undertakings were achieving throughout the land.[9]

Finney's theology not only reflected the current situation in America, but also the theological developments which preceded him. His theology was not something entirely new, nor was it unique to Finney. He was but one proponent of a theological approach which was the culmination of a gradual development within New England theology. This development, described as an ascent by one historian[10] and a descent by another,[11] began with Jonathan Edwards, even though it was a movement away from his strict Calvinism. Within his framework of determinism, Edwards did affirm the freedom of the will, at least on a psychological level. Edward's view provided a starting point for later New England thinkers to move away from his determinism.

This development began with the "New Divinity" movement led by Edward's students and interpreters, men such as Joseph Bellamy, Samuel Hopkins, Nathanael Emmons, and Jonathan Edwards, Jr. Bellamy (1719–1790) paved the way for the theology of Finney with an emphasis on God as "moral governor," sin as actions rather than nature, God's wrath as governmental rather than personal, and the atonement as general rather than limited. Samuel Hopkins (1721–1803) provided the definitions of sin and virtue Finney would later adopt: sin as selfishness and virtue as disinterested benevolence. Hopkins further stressed the individual's active role in conversion, though he maintained that this followed regeneration, in which the individual is passive. Emmons (1745–1840) emphasized that sin consisted not of a disposition, or nature, but of acts of the will. Jonathan Edwards, Jr. (1745–1801) developed and advocated a governmental theory of the atonement, a view introduced into New England theology by Bellamy. These men, while not departing from Edward's determinism, in their modifications of his thought broke ground for those who would.

Because of its center at Yale, the movement within New England theology taking that decisive step came to be called the New Haven theology. The founder of the New Haven theology was Timothy Dwight (1758–1817), but its real architect was Nathaniel William Taylor (1786–1858), whose theological system viewed the individual as a free moral agent under the moral government of God. Other proponents of this view included Lyman Beecher (1775–1863) and Albert Barnes (1798–1870). All of these men were either Presbyterians or Congregationalists, and their thought came to be called the "New School" theology among those churches.

The center of opposition to the New School was at Princeton. The "Old School" Calvinists found leadership in Archibald Alexander (1772–1878) and Charles Hodge (1797–1878). These men built their understanding and defense of Calvinism, not upon Edwards, but the seventeenth-century Scholastic, Francois Turretin. Both Hodge and a later Princetonian, Benjamin Warfield, wrote critiques of Finney's theology.[12] The division between Old and New School eventually led to a collapse of the Presbyterian-Congregationalist cooperative union and to an internal split within Presbyterianism that lasted from 1837 to 1869.

Finney's theology clearly followed the New School tradition. In fact, he was the most radical in stating that theology and the most successful in practically applying its ideas. Finney's theology was very close to that of Taylor's, yet Finney claimed to have developed his thought independently. He did not express any indebtedness to the New Divinity men. Any references to them are almost uniformly critical. He grouped them all with the Old School and seemed to be unaware of the subtle ways in which they shaped his own theology. Nor did Finney have any extensive contact with the men of the New Haven theology. One of the New School leaders, Beecher, initially opposed Finney. The fact that Finney could independently develop a theology so close to that of Taylor and others simply illustrates that his thought was a natural evolution within New England theology, as well as a natural product of Jacksonian America.[13]

The opposition Finney faced included not only Old School Calvinists but also rationalists of various sorts such as Deists, Unitarians, and Universalists. In his preaching and theology, Finney, like others in the New School, sought to meet these movements on their own ground—reason. "Our reason," Finney wrote, "was given us for the very purpose of justifying the ways of God."[14] In order to show the reasonableness of scriptural Christianity, Finney, like many of his day, adopted the approach of the Scottish Common Sense Philosophy developed by Thomas Reid and Dugald Stewart. This philosophy argued that the basic beliefs of intuition, reason, and observation common to everyone were to be relied upon. From this approach Finney and the other New School theologians would argue that all people are conscious that they are free moral agents. For these theologians there was no inconsistency between reason and revelation and the perspicuity of both nature and Scripture was affirmed. While perhaps not consciously borrowing from this school of thought, Finney definitely adopted this approach, common in his day, and used it to erect his rational system and practical preaching. His preaching aimed at convincing sinners of the reasonableness of obedience and the "moral insanity" of sin.[15] Having described the environment in which Finney's theology developed, let us describe briefly the theological system itself.

FINNEY'S THEOLOGICAL SYSTEM

In Finney's theological system, God's relationship to humanity is understood in terms of God's moral government. God governs, not by means of physical force, but by means of moral influence. By means of the law and its sanctions and through appeals to humanity's will through the revelation of Scripture, God seeks to direct men and women to obey his moral law. God's laws are not arbitrary but are the laws of reason and nature. What God requires is benevolence or good will in general, or choosing the highest well-being of God and the universe. Righteousness, then, is to live exclusively for the promotion of the happiness of God and one's fellow. Sin, on the other hand, is selfishness or supreme self-interest. In Finney's theology, everyone exists as a free moral agent with the natural ability and, therefore, the responsibility to submit to God's government and obey his law. Since all are, by choice, sinners, all need to turn from selfishness to benevolence.

The atonement is presented by Finney as a satisfaction of public justice, a means by which God could display his opposition to sin and yet show mercy to repentant sinners. In this way, mercy could be offered without undermining confidence in his government. This atonement also becomes the most powerful influence within God's government to lead men and women to repentance and obedience.

The task of the revivalist, then, is to be a co-worker with God. First, he must show the sinner his great guilt as a rebel against God's government. Then, he must direct and exhort the sinner to repent, to submit to God's law, to turn from selfishness to benevolence, and to place faith in Christ's atonement as the only hope of forgiveness. It is vital to this system, and the revivalist's task, to emphasize the individual's responsibility for his sinful character and his freedom to repent. Out of this emphasis on personal freedom and a moralistic understanding of salvation developed Finney's understanding of the possibility of Christian perfection, which will be described more fully later in this study.[16]

Finney was concerned, not only to develop a theological system, but moreover, to convert and sanctify sinners. This practical concern enabled Finney to see, from the onset of his ministry, the power of selfishness and the actual moral inability of individuals to change themselves, despite their theoretical natural ability. Finney recognized that only the powerful influence of the Holy Spirit could convert and sanctify sinners. Only preachers energized by the Spirit could be effective co-workers with God. It was out of this awareness that Finney developed his doctrine of the Baptism in the Spirit.

Finney's understanding of this doctrine reflects the same cultural and theological roots as his theology as a whole, described above.

The understanding of the gospel as the means of making individuals moral, and the optimistic millennial hope which grew out of these influences, both lead to the practical questions of how are ministers to be empowered so as to be successful in converting sinners and, once converted, how are Christians to be established in sanctification. In other words, How is the perfection of individuals and society to be achieved? It was in answer to such questions that Finney developed his doctrine of the Baptism in the Holy Spirit. Where Finney and his colleagues at Oberlin differed from theologians before them was in affirming that this Baptism was an experience distinct from and subsequent to conversion.

THE BAPTISM IN THE SPIRIT IN

FINNEY'S LIFE AND WRITINGS

B EFORE DISCUSSING THE VARIOUS ASPECTS of Finney's doctrine of the Baptism in the Spirit in depth, one must give a general overview of the subject as it developed in Finney's experience and understanding. Such a survey is necessitated by the fact that many references to Finney's view are often misleading or, at best, incomplete. B. B. Warfield, for example, in his critique of Oberlin theology and other Perfectionist movements, claimed that Finney "dallied a little with the idea of the Baptism of the Spirit, but did not really adopt it."[1] More recently Donald Dayton stated that the earliest discussion on the Baptism in the Spirit by Finney that he was aware of was in 1871, when Finney was 79 years old![2] Timothy L. Smith, on the other hand, has shown that Finney had definitely developed a doctrine of the Baptism in the Spirit by 1840.[3] What Smith failed to recognize, however, is how much of Finney's doctrine was already implicitly present in his earlier writings. All the basic components of Finney's view existed in his first major published work, *Revival Lectures*. Further, as was stated in the introduction, Smith's discussion of Finney's view revolves around its relationship to sanctification; the fact that Finney also gave prominent attention to the role of this Baptism in empowering for ministry is left unmentioned.

Related to the development of Finney's theology of the Baptism in the Spirit is the question of the time of his own experience of this baptism. Smith, along with McLoughlin, points to an experience in the winter of 1843–44 described in Finney's autobiography as the time of his Spirit Baptism.[4] I will show, however, that Finney actually pointed to an earlier experience immediately following his conversion as his Baptism in the Holy Spirit.

In the following survey, then, I will demonstrate that Finney experienced the Baptism in the Spirit at the beginning of his Christian life, and though an explicit statement of his doctrine and the use of the phrase "Baptism of the Spirit" would not occur until 1839–40, a basic understanding was latent in his early thought. Furthermore, I will show the dual emphasis upon sanctification and empowering in Finney's writings. We will look at his major writings and the important sermons, articles, and tracts in which the Baptism in the Spirit is discussed.

FINNEY'S BAPTISM IN THE SPIRIT

Finney's Baptism in the Spirit immediately following his conversion is described in his autobiography. This began, when Finney, having become convinced of the truth of the gospel as a result of reading the Bible in relation to his law studies, faced the question of his own response to God. One October morning in 1821, determined to "give his heart to God and place his faith in Christ for salvation," Finney isolated himself in the woods to pray. After a great struggle and a revelation of his own sinfulness and pride, Finney humbled himself and cried out to the Lord, putting his faith in the promises of Scripture that, it seemed to him, God was placing before his mind. Immediately Finney experienced a great peace, a complete absence of any feelings of condemnation, and an overflowing love for God.[5] At the time, Finney did not even realize that he had been converted. Only later was he to understand this experience in the woods as the point of his regeneration.[6]

That evening, Finney remained alone in the law office to pray. Before he even began to pray, however, he experienced a vision of Jesus Christ standing before him. In his own words:

> It seemed to me that I saw Him as I would see any other man. He said nothing but looked at me in such a manner as to break me right down at His feet. I have always since regarded this as a most remarkable state of mind; for it seemed to me a reality, that He stood before me, and I fell down at His feet and poured out my soul to Him.[7]

After some time of praying "at the feet of Jesus," Finney retired to another room of the law office. There, he immediately received what he would describe in his autobiography as "a mighty baptism of the Holy Ghost."[8] It is best to give Finney's own description of this experience.

> The Holy Spirit descended upon me in a manner that seemed to go through me body and soul. I could feel the impression like a wave of electricity, going through and through me. Indeed it seemed to come in

waves and waves of liquid love, for I could not express it in any other way. It seemed like the very breath of God. I can recollect distinctly that it seemed to fan me, like immense wings.

No words can express the wonderful love that was shed abroad in my heart. I wept aloud with joy and love; and I do not know but I should say I literally bellowed out the unutterable gushings of my heart. These waves came over me, one after the other until I recollect I cried out, "I shall die if these waves continue to pass over me," I said, "Lord, I cannot bear any more" yet I had no fear of death.[9]

A member of the church came by the law office and upon hearing Finney's loud weeping asked if he were in pain. Finney replied, "No, but so happy that I cannot live."[10]

Those who point to a later experience as Finney's Baptism in the Spirit understand the description above as referring, not to some experience subsequent to his conversion, but as itself part of his conversion experience.[11] However, Finney stated, quite clearly, in another writing:

I was powerfully converted on the morning of the tenth of October. In the evening of the same day, I received overwhelming baptisms of the Holy Ghost, that went through me as it seemed to me body and soul.[12]

The context of this statement is an article on the Baptism in the Spirit as an enduement of power distinct from and subsequent to conversion. Thus, it is clear that Finney did not regard this experience as part of his conversion.

This is further evident from a careful reading of his autobiography. Finney states there that he received this baptism

without any expectation of it, without ever having the thought in mind that there was any such thing for me, without any recollection that I had ever heard the thing mentioned by any person in the world.[13]

Finney was familiar with the concept of regeneration or conversion and surely he had heard testimonies of such experiences, but he was completely ignorant of the experience of the Baptism in the Spirit, inasmuch as this was unheard of in the church of his day. Later in his autobiography, he refers to the possibility of being converted and yet, still be lacking this Baptism of the Holy Spirit.[14]

Other students of Finney's life and theology have recognized this experience following his conversion as his initial Baptism in the Spirit.[15] In fact, one of Finney's biographers, a former Oberlin student and a Holiness preacher, educator, and theologian, A. M. Hills, marveled at Finney's experience. He wrote:

I question if there is a parallel to this in all the literature of the saints—a man receiving such a Baptism with the Spirit so soon after conversion, without asking for it or expecting it, and when he was too utterly ignorant of the whole subject to even think about it.[16]

Finney's autobiography describes another, later baptism in the Spirit, which brought him into a higher level of Christian experience than he had previously attained.[17] It is that experience which Smith and McLoughlin have mistakenly identified as Finney's "second blessing" or Baptism in the Spirit. Finney himself referred to this experience as a "*fresh* baptism of His Spirit."[18] Though this experience was for Finney a Baptism in the Spirit, it was not his initial such experience.

A. M. Hills, writing from his Holiness perspective, claimed that Finney received the Baptism in the Holy Spirit immediately following his conversion, yet admitted that this later experience was also "a sanctifying Baptism with the Holy Ghost."[19] He explained this by suggesting that Finney had lost the "fullness of the blessing" received in his initial baptism, that this blessing had "leaked away," and Finney found himself, once again, in need of the Baptism in the Spirit.

This second Baptism can be better explained from Finney's own perspective. He viewed the Baptism, not as a once-and-for-all unrepeatable experience, but as something which the Christian required again and again.[20] He saw the Christian life as involving a series of Baptisms in the Spirit, bringing the believer into ever-higher levels of Christian experience.[21] This aspect of Finney's view will be discussed more fully below.

Having established the fact that Finney received the Baptism in the Holy Spirit immediately following his conversion, we must point out that it would be some time later before his understanding of this doctrine would develop, and the Baptism in the Spirit would occupy a prominent place in his preaching and writing. When we read his description of his own Spirit Baptism, we must remember that this was not written until 1868, forty-seven years later, and that it reflects his understanding as it later developed.

THE EVOLUTION OF FINNEY'S
DOCTRINE OF THE BAPTISM OF THE SPIRIT

In Finney's earliest recorded sermons, we find no mention of the Baptism in the Spirit.[22] However, this may be accounted for by the fact that his early ministry was devoted entirely to evangelism. His efforts were focused on converting sinners—both within and without the church. Finney later admitted that he erred in neglecting to direct efforts toward the sanctification and growth in grace of the saints and especially in failing to ensure that new converts receive the Baptism in the Holy Spirit.[23]

It was not until 1839–1840, after directing his attention toward the needs of Christians rather than the unconverted, that Finney developed an understanding of the Baptism in the Spirit. This is illustrated by one of his comments, written in 1840:

> The fact that the baptism of the Holy Ghost is a thing universally promised or profferred to Christians under this dispensation, and that this blessing is to be sought and received after conversion, was not so distinctly before my mind formerly as it has been of late. I am satisfied that this truth is abundantly taught in the Bible.[24]

Though his own view did not crystallize within his mind until 1839–1840, it would be a mistake to see the Baptism in the Spirit as a novel addition to his earlier theology; rather, it is a clarification and more explicit expression of ideas already present in his theology. His early experience of the Spirit profoundly influenced Finney's theology from the very beginning, and the doctrine of the Baptism in the Spirit that he ultimately developed was the fruit of a gradual development rather than the sudden adoption of a new idea. This is best illustrated by Finney's *Lectures on Revivals of Religion*.[25]

Lectures on Revivals of Religion

Finney gave these lectures in New York in 1834, and they were recorded and published in *The New York Evangelist*. They were published in book form soon after. By that time, Finney's success in promoting revivals had been proven not only in the frontier towns of western New York, but in New York City and other major cities as well. Thus, though he had his many critics, many others were eager to know his views on revivals in order to adopt them in promoting such movements in their own churches. This book was welcomed by many as a textbook for revivals written by a master revivalist.

The most striking aspect of this work for most commentators is not Finney's emphasis on the role of the Spirit of God in revivals, but rather his emphasis upon the role of the individual. William McLoughlin, for example, finds the "brief acknowledgement of the supernatural element in revivals" so "buried" beneath instructions in the certain "scientific measures" men may adopt in the promotion of revivals that Finney's lectures end up presenting man as "omnipotent" in the sphere of revivals.[26]

At first glance, this view seems justified. Finney claimed that "religion is the work of man."[27] He argued that there were means men could employ in promoting revival which would ensure success. Just as the farmer went about his business of plowing and planting with the confidence that, given proper weather, he would definitely reap a harvest, so Christians could go about the business of promoting revival with an assurance that there was a connection between means and results. If they practiced the proper means, as instructed by Finney, they could achieve the desired result—revival.

Before pronouncing Finney as Pelagian, however, one must carefully consider the measures Finney suggests for the promotion of revivals. The measure foremost in Finney's mind was prayer for the outpouring of the Spirit. Religion was the work of man, Finney said, but he immediately added, God "induces him to do it."[28] It was up to individuals to preach and pray and labor for the conversion of sinners. Yet, all this work for revival is in vain without the influence of the Holy Spirit. Finney urged his readers to

> have high ideas of the Holy Ghost, and to feel that nothing good will be done without His influences. No praying or preaching will be of any avail, without Him. If Jesus Christ were to come down here and preach to sinners, not one would be converted without the Spirit.[29]

Finney was no Pelagian, but he was well aware of the need for the inner work of the Holy Spirit to effect conversion. "Unless God interpose the influence of His Spirit," Finney wrote, "not a man on earth will ever obey the commands of God."[30] The reason that people will not repent apart from the influence of the Spirit, according to Finney, is their own sinful rebellion against God and opposition to his demands upon their life. It is only the Holy Spirit who can gain access to their inner minds and there present the truths of the gospel with such force as to induce sinners to repent and believe the gospel. Finney wrote:

> If men were disposed to obey God, the truth is given with sufficient clearness in the Bible and from preaching they could learn all that is necessary for them to know. But because they are wholly disinclined to obey it, God makes it clear before their minds, and pours in upon their souls a blaze of convincing light, which they cannot withstand and they yield to it, obey God, and are saved.[31]

It is clear from such passages in the *Lectures on Revivals of Religion*, that, for Finney, the indispensable ingredient for revival was the outpouring of the Holy Spirit. The most important means, then, in promoting revival was that which secured this outpouring—prayer. G. F. Wright wrote that Finney

> believed also that nothing could be effected in promoting a revival of religion except through prayer, and by the special aid of the Spirit. His first aim, therefore was always to secure united prayer for the outpouring of the Spirit.[32]

This biographer described Finney's practice in his earliest revivals in which he would always begin his labors in a particular place by gathering together whatever praying Christians there were and joining them in prayer for the Spirit to be poured out.[33]

Finney's assurance that the use of the proper means would always produce revival was based not on his confidence in human ability but rather on his faith in God's willingness to pour out his Spirit for the purpose of converting sinners. Prayer and other means which Christians could use to promote revival did not somehow alter God's will but simply put the Christians themselves in such a state in which it was proper for God to bless them and their efforts to convert sinners, as he was already desiring to do.[34] McLoughlin, somewhat at odds with his comment quoted earlier, recognized, too, the source of Finney's optimism.

> His optimism lay not so much in his faith in man as in his faith that God's transcendent power over the world, the flesh, and the devil was readily available to man.[35]

This transcendent power of God is made readily available to humanity in the person of the Holy Spirit.

Thus far, we have demonstrated that Finney's lectures on revivals did not merely stress the individual's role in revivals, they also taught that sinners could not be converted apart from the agency of the Holy Spirit, and that Christians needed to pray for a general outpouring of the Spirit in order to see revival come and sinners converted. Finney's doctrine of the Baptism in the Spirit, as it later developed, however, was more than simply an affirmation of the Spirit's role in conversion or revival. The Baptism was viewed as a distinct experience in the life of the individual Christian subsequent to conversion. We find this concept as well in Finney's *Lectures on Revivals*, only without the expression "Baptism in the Spirit." In this earlier period Finney favored the term "filling of the Spirit," but all the other basic components of his later doctrine are present in these lectures.

In these lectures Finney gave extensive attention to the subject of "being filled with the Spirit" in which he urged upon Christians their need for the Holy Spirit. He presents the abiding, indwelling presence of the Spirit as something for which Christians are to pray.[36] Many Christians are not "filled with the Spirit" or do not "have the Spirit." A "Christian" without the Spirit may indeed not be a real Christian at all. If he is, and if he continues without the Spirit, he will surely not remain a Christian. Those Christians who oppose revivals and the use of measures to promote them are, according to Finney, clearly without the Spirit.[37]

Finney's view at this time may be summarized as follows: whereas sinners become Christians by the agency of the Holy Spirit and are consequently indwelt by him, there are many who are Christians who do not "have the Spirit" in the sense of knowing in their own experience what it is to be filled with the Spirit. To be filled with the Spirit is to experience the Spirit as an abiding, indwelling presence who imparts peace within one's soul, victory in one's life, and wisdom and power in securing the conversion of sinners.[38] The Spirit-filled Christian knows the Spirit especially as the "Spirit of Prayer" and experiences his influence in his prayers.[39] Thus, Christians are to pray for the Holy Spirit and persevere in prayer until they receive.

The Christian needs the Spirit for two reasons: first, for personal sanctification, and second, for becoming useful in doing God's work in the world.[40] The Spirit is not given merely to make the Christian happy, though he does impart great peace and joy. "A Christian should pray for the Spirit that he may be the more useful and glorify God more, not that he himself may be more happy."[41]

Finney's later discussions of the Baptism in the Holy Spirit revolved around those two themes: sanctification and usefulness. The Baptism was presented either as a cleansing, liberating experience or as an experience of empowerment for ministry. Finney would also continue to emphasize the Spirit as "the Spirit of Prayer," which can be considered as one aspect of his empowering. The basis for the Spirit's sanctifying and empowering, in Finney's understanding, was the fact that the Spirit unites believers to Christ in an experiential way. This idea, too, was present as early as Finney's *Revival Letters*. He stated there that through the influence of the Holy Spirit, particularly in prayer,

> it is as if Christ came and poured the overflowings of His own benevolent heart into His people and lead them to co-operate with Him as they never do in any other way.[42]

Lectures to Professing Christians

The crucial years in the development of Finney's view were 1839–1840. During this time he began to devote his attention more towards the sanctification of Christians rather than the conversion of sinners. This concern was expressed earlier in his *Lectures to Professing Christians*, first preached in the winters of 1835–1836 and 1836–1837. It was at that time that Finney began to urge Christians to go on to perfection. While not claiming to have yet attained this state himself, Finney did see it as attainable.[43] In fact, he claimed that "the perfect sanctification of believers is the very object for which the Holy Spirit is promised."[44] The stage is set in these lectures for Finney's later presentation of the Baptism in the Holy Spirit as the means to Christian perfection. Even at this time, Finney was urging his readers to recognize their dependence on the Holy Spirit and to exercise their faith and yield to the Spirit's sanctifying work:

> Instead of taking scriptural views of their dependence and seeing where their strength is and realizing how willing God is to give His Holy Spirit to them that ask now and continually and thus taking hold and holding on by the arm of God, they sit down in unbelief and sin to wait God's time and call this depending on God. Alas how little is felt, after all this talk about dependence on the Holy Spirit; how little is there of giving up of the whole soul to his control and guidance, with faith in his power to enlighten, to lead, to sanctify, to kindle the affections, and fill the soul continuously with all the fullness of God.[45]

While these sermons were given in New York City, the background to them is found at Oberlin. From 1835 to 1837 Finney spent his summers teaching at Oberlin and the rest of the year pastoring in New York City. In the college's second year, September 1836, a student asked the president of the college, Asa Mahan, if a life of perfect sanctification, of unbroken peace uninterrupted by sin and condemnation, was attainable in this life. Mahan's answer was yes.[46] Finney and the other professors at Oberlin had taught that regeneration implied a real change of heart and life, and that the Christian life was one characterized by victory over sin. Now, these professors turned their attention to the question of how to attain the state in which this victory would be continual, without any interruption by sin.

For Finney, his investigation into this subject grew out of a dissatisfaction with his own spiritual state and a hunger for a higher experience, as well as a desire to lead the converts from his various revivals and others into a higher Christian life.[47] Finney's desires for his own experience seemed to have been answered. He wrote that during the last winter spent as a pastor in New York City, 1836–1837, "the Lord was pleased to visit my soul with a great refreshing. After a season of great searching of heart, he brought me, as he has often done, into a large place, and gave me much of that divine sweetness in my soul." His spiritual experiences of that time "resulted in the great renewal of my spiritual strength, and enlargement of my views in regard to the privileges of Christians, and the abundance of the grace of God."[48] Later, in 1839, Finney would write that, whereas before he knew Christ "almost exclusively as an atoning and justifying Savior" he had come to know him as "a Jesus to save men from sin, or as a sanctifying Savior" and consequently "felt as strongly and unequivocally pressed by the Spirit of God to labor for the sanctification of the church as I once did for the conversion of sinners."[49]

·Finney and the other theological professors at Oberlin, Asa Mahan, Henry Cowles, and John Morgan, began promoting their views on sanctification among the public in their periodical, *The Oberlin Evangelist,* which was initially published in 1839. It was in a series of articles appearing in 1839–1840 that Finney began explicitly to present the Baptism in the Holy Spirit as the means of entire or permanent sanctification.[50]

Articles of 1839–1840

Included in these lectures were several on the "promises of God," appearing in the summer of 1839. These focused especially on those promises associated with the new covenant, such as Jer. 31:31–34, Ezk. 36:25–27, and Heb. 8:7–11. In these passages one finds God's promises to give his people a new heart, to put his Spirit within them, to write his laws upon their hearts and to cause them to walk in his ways. According to Finney, the new covenant is "the effectual indwelling of the Holy Spirit, producing the very temper required by the law or Old Covenant."[51] The promise of the new covenant includes something beyond regeneration. The Old Testament saints were regenerated, according to Finney, but the Book of Hebrews states that they "died in faith not having received the promises" (Heb. 11:13).[52] As Finney understood it, "the thing that Abraham and the Old Testament saints did not receive was the measure of the Holy Spirit which constitutes the New Covenant and produces the entire sanctification of the soul."[53] This is the blessing of Abraham which comes on the Gentiles through Jesus Christ (Gal. 3:14), the Holy Spirit of Promise by whom Christians are sealed after they have believed

(Eph. 1:13).[54] Finney emphasized that the passage in Ephesians states that *"after* that ye believed ye were sealed with that Holy Spirit of Promise" (KJV). Thus, this baptism of the Spirit which sanctifies the soul is received after regeneration. This blessing was made available to the entire church at Pentecost, but it remains for each individual Christian to personally obtain this blessing by faith.[55] Therefore,

> every individual Christian may receive and is bound to receive this gift of the Holy Ghost through faith at the present moment. It must not be supposed that every Christian has of course received the Holy Spirit in such a sense as is promised in these passages of Scripture.[56]

In 1840 Finney published in the *Oberlin Evangelist* two letters to "ministers of the gospel of all denominations" in which he emphasized the importance of the Baptism in the Holy Spirit. In the first, he stressed the need for the new convert to "seek earnestly the baptism of the Holy Ghost after that he has believed" for this Baptism is "the secret of the stability of Christian character." He admitted that his own instructions to converts had been lacking in this regard as he had not clearly recognized that "this blessing is to be sought and received after conversion." Now, however, Finney was certain that "this truth is abundantly taught in the Bible."[57]

In the second letter, Finney stressed the importance that ministers be baptized with the Holy Spirit. In this context he stressed not the sanctifying effects of this Baptism, but its empowering. This was the one needful thing, more important than ministerial education, that the minister of the gospel be "endued with power from on high," that he receive this "anointing" which would give him "power with God or man." The "main design and bearing" of this Baptism for the apostles at Pentecost, as well as ministers today, "was to fill them with light and love and power in preaching the gospel."[58]

Also in 1840 Finney wrote a series of articles on sanctification which were later published as a booklet entitled *Views On Sanctification.*[59] Much of this material was later incorporated in his *Systematic Theology.* In these articles Finney does not specifically mention the Baptism in the Spirit, though he does refer to the promised outpouring of the Holy Spirit in Joel 2:28 and the sealing of the Spirit in Eph. 1:13 in connection with entire sanctification.[60] This experience of sanctification was presented as something more than and subsequent to regeneration. Entire sanctification, Finney wrote in one of these articles, is possible under the gospel dispensation because believers now have available to them a greater amount of the Spirit's influence. The Holy Spirit sanctifies by revealing Christ to the soul and giving that true knowledge of God which alone can produce true love and purity in the heart.[61]

In the summer of 1840, Finney specifically mentioned the Baptism in the Spirit as the means of sanctification in his sermon on "Death to Sin." Death to sin, he wrote, "consists in the annihilation of selfishness and the reign of perfect love to God and man in the heart and life." Such a state of mind is effected by the Baptism of the Holy Spirit. In this Baptism, the believer receives "such a degree of divine influence as will purify the heart." This Baptism is a "spiritual baptism into Christ's death" which delivers from the power of sin. The Baptism in the Spirit is not a one-time, unrepeatable experience, for "renewed temptation calls for fresh and more powerful Baptisms of the Holy Spirit." Christians should look to God daily for "deeper draughts of the water of life."[62]

A Fresh Baptism in the Spirit

This idea of fresh and repeated Baptisms of the Spirit was part of Finney's own experience. It was one such rebaptism in the winter of 1843–1844 which has been mistakenly described as Finney's initial Baptism in the Spirit. Finney recorded in his autobiography that "during this winter, the Lord gave my own soul a very thorough overhauling and fresh baptism of His Spirit."[63] Finney's description of this fresh Baptism is very similar to later Wesleyan-Holiness descriptions of the second blessing and this probably accounts for the erroneous interpretations.[64] Indeed, according to Finney, this experience brought him into a higher level of Christian living than he had heretofore experienced in an abiding way. He described the results of this experience as follows:

> I can come to God with more calmness, because with more perfect confidence. [sic] He enables me now to rest in him, and let everything sink into his perfect will, with much more readiness, than ever before the experience of that winter. I have felt since then a religious freedom, a religious bouyancy and delight in God, and in His Word, a steadiness of faith, a Christian liberty and overflowing love that I had only experienced, I may say, occasionally before.[65]

This fresh Baptism of the Spirit brought Finney into a deeper experience of union with Christ.

> At this time it seemed as if my soul was wedded to Christ, in a sense in which I had never had any thought or conception. The language of the Song of Solomon was as natural to me as my breath.[66]

While this experience was the most extensively described, there are references to other similar experiences in Finney's memoirs. I have already mentioned the experience during his last winter in New York in which he claimed, "The Lord was pleased to visit my soul with a great refreshing"[67] and, of course, his first Baptism in the Spirit following his conversion.

In a sermon on the "Essential Elements of Christian Experience," Finney described the Christian life as one of "impulsive progression." A time of intense spiritual desire and hunger and thirst for righteousness leads to a time of the soul being filled to overflowing with the Spirit. The believer gains a greater vision of God and experiences a new and deeper union with Christ, bringing him into a higher level of Christian living than before. It is a mistake, however, to suggest that after this experience the Christian will never again hunger and thirst spiritually. After a time of enjoying this spiritual plateau, the Christian will begin once again to desire greatly an even higher experience with God. This desire will lead to another fresh Baptism leading into that higher experience. This process of "impulsive progression," Finney suggests, may continue even in heaven."[68]

While these so-called essential elements may not describe every Christian's experience, this sermon is obviously a description of Finney's own experience. Finney's understanding of repeated Baptisms must be taken into account by any historian who would try to identify any one experience in Finney's life as his "second blessing," "Baptism in the Spirit," or "entire sanctification."

Writings: 1845–1855

In 1845–1846 Finney wrote a second series of letters on revivals in the *Oberlin Evangelist* in which he shared his thoughts, observations, and experiences concerning revivals during the approximately ten years since the publication of his original *Lectures on Revivals of Religion*.[69] In his introduction to a recent republication of these letters, Donald Dayton summarizes their basic purpose and content:

> These letters contain Finney's mature reflections on revivals. They were designed to correct some of his own earlier emphases and attempted to counteract both the resistance to revivals that dominated some quarters and the extremes that had developed in others. They also sought to deal with the problem of "backsliders" by calling converts to further spiritual growth and "a higher Christian life."[70]

One new emphasis within these letters is that ministers need to be baptized with the Holy Spirit.[71]

In Finney's *Systematic Theology*, first published in 1846–1847, one finds no stress upon the Baptism in the Spirit, though it contains an extensive discussion of sanctification. In the discussion of sanctification Finney stresses the agency of Christ rather than the Holy Spirit. He emphasizes the believer's relationship to Christ as his sanctification. Finney uses the terms entire or permanent sanctification rather than Baptism in the Spirit. Because of this, prior to Timothy Smith's research, many scholars relying upon Finney's *Systematic Theology* failed to recognize that he did indeed believe in the Baptism in the Spirit as the means to entire sanctification at this stage of his career.[72]

If one reads Finney's *Systematic Theology* carefully, however, one finds examples of this belief. He claims that "the Holy Spirit is given to Christians to abide with them and in them, for the express purpose of procuring entire sanctification in this life."[73] This sanctification comes through "so rich an anointing of the Holy Spirit" that the believer is "so thoroughly baptized into the death of Christ as to remain henceforth in a state of abiding consecration to God."[74] The Old Testament saints did not receive this experience of sanctification for it is only now in the Christian dispensation that the Spirit of Promise is given. This is the fulfillment of Joel's prophecy that the Spirit would be poured out on all flesh, and the prophecy of John the Baptist, repeated by Jesus just prior to Pentecost, that "ye shall be baptized with the Holy Spirit." Entire sanctification is possible to Christians because to them is offered the "fullness of the Spirit."[75] This is the "sealing of the Spirit which Christians receive after regeneration."[76] All that Christians need to be holy, Finney writes in his *Systematic Theology*, is to "receive the Holy Spirit."[77] Finney combines christological and pneumatological emphases. Sanctification, he wrote, is "by the Holy Spirit or Spirit of Christ, or which is the same thing, by Christ our sanctification, living and reigning in the heart."[78] So, while Finney's *Systematic Theology* stresses the believer's need to appropriate Christ as his sanctification, there is an equal emphasis that it is through the Holy Spirit that this union with Christ comes about. Thus, as we have demonstrated by the above references, even in this work—though the phrase "Baptism in the Spirit" is only once mentioned,[79] Finney does present sanctification as coming through the appropriation of the fullness of the Spirit.

Two important sermons on the Baptism in the Spirit appeared in the *Oberlin Evangelist* in the 1850s and were later published in two of the collections of Finney's sermons. The first, appearing in 1853, was the aforementioned sermon on the "Essential Elements of Christian Experience." In that sermon Finney discusses that deeper work of the Spirit following conversion which brings the believer into a higher Christian experience and which ought to be repeated throughout the course of life. He refers to this experience as "a baptism, an anointing, an unction, an ensealing of the Spirit, an earnest of the Spirit. All of these terms are pertinent and beautiful to denote this special work of the Divine Spirit in the soul."[80]

The second sermon appearing in 1855 was entitled "On Prayer for the Holy Spirit," and was based upon Luke 11:13:

> If ye then, being evil, know how to give good gifts to your children how much more shall your heavenly Father give the Holy Spirit to them that ask Him.

The phrase "Baptism in the Spirit" does not occur, but it is clear that Finney has in mind this post-conversion experience. Jesus' words are addressed to Christians. It is they who are encouraged to pray for the Holy Spirit. Christians do indeed have the Spirit. In fact, the total consecration which precedes this experience implies "a large measure of the Spirit" but not yet the "largest measure." When the Christian received the "Spirit of God in fullest measure" he will experience "a deep union with God . . . a consciousness of God in the soul." To be filled with the Spirit means not only to possess the fullness of the Spirit but also for the Spirit to possess fully the believer. "To be filled with the Holy Ghost, so that he takes full possession of our souls, is what I mean by sanctification." In this sermon Finney particularly emphasizes that the Holy Spirit is given to unite us with God. The "gift of the Holy Spirit comprehends all that we need spiritually," for it secures to us that union with God which is eternal life and sanctification. It is the Spirit's "business" to bring about a state of

> complete union and sympathy between our souls and God, so that the soul should enjoy God's own peace and should be in complete harmony with its maker and Father.[81]

Memoirs

In his memoirs written in 1867–1868, Finney emphasized the importance of ministers being empowered by God through the baptism in the Holy Spirit. Rather than an actual autobiography, Finney intended this work to be a history of the revivals in which he had labored. In his description of those revivals he wished to stress "the manifest agency of the Holy Spirit . . . underlying, directing, and giving efficiency to the means, without which nothing would be accomplished."[82] Finney attributed the success of his revival preaching to the anointing of the Holy Spirit which he had received.[83] When he recalled his early theological education under the tutelage of his pastor, "Brother Gale," Finney described how erroneous he believed this Old School Calvinist's views were. However, the most "fundamental defect" Finney found in this pastor's ministerial preparation was that "he had failed to receive that divine anointing of the Holy Ghost that would make him a power in the pulpit and society for the conversion of souls. He had fallen short of receiving the baptism of the Holy Ghost which is indispensable to ministerial success."[84] Finney pointed to the example of the apostles, who, when commissioned by Christ to preach, were told to wait in Jerusalem for the enduement of power from on high which came upon them when they were baptized with the Holy Ghost on the Day of Pentecost. This Baptism

> was a divine purifying, an anointing bestowing upon them a divine illumination, filling them with faith and love, with peace and power; so that their words were made sharp in the hearts of God's enemies, quick and powerful like a two-edged sword.[85]

The lack of this power continued to be a problem in the ministry to the current day, Finney wrote. He felt that the church did not lay enough stress on the importance of the Baptism in the Spirit for preaching the gospel to sinners.

One also finds examples of Finney's belief in the Baptism in the Spirit as the means of entire sanctification in his memoirs. He describes there the experience of the very godly Christian wife of an unconverted man who was hungry for a "deeper work of grace in her soul." After receiving what Finney described as "the sealing of the Holy Spirit" and "a fresh baptism of the Holy Spirit" she exhibited "such a change, such an energy in her religion, such a fullness of joy and peace and love" that her husband, who had already "thought her almost or quite perfect," was totally astounded.[86]

Tracts on Spirit Baptism

In several tracts written in the last years of his life, Finney spoke about the Baptism in the Spirit.[87] Two of these tracts were directed toward preachers. One entitled "Preacher Save Thyself," based upon 1 Tim. 4:16, was simply a list of brief exhortations to ministers. The second exhortation in this list reads, "See that you have the special enduement of power from on high by the Baptism of the Holy Ghost."[88] A second tract provided preachers with advice on "How to Win Souls." In that tract Finney claimed that

> a truly successful preacher must not only win souls to Christ, but must keep them won. He must not only secure their conversion, but their permanent sanctification.

This permanent sanctification, promised in 1 Thes. 5:23–24, comes when the believer, after regeneration, is "sealed with the Holy Spirit of Promise" according to Eph. 1:13–14. "The baptism or sealing of the Holy Spirit subdues the power of the desires and strengthens and confirms the will in resisting the impulse of desire, and in abiding permanently in a state of making the whole being an offering to God." This "sealing" renders one's salvation sure. It is of "utmost importance" that ministers know this experience themselves and lead converts into it. To fail to do so is to "leave out the very cream and fullness of the gospel."[89]

Several other tracts grew out of an address Finney delivered to the First National Congregational Council, meeting in Oberlin in November 1871. Finney, then nearly 80 years old, addressed those gathered there on "The Enduement of the Holy Ghost."[90] This address and further articles on the theme were subsequently published in the New York *Independent*. They later appeared separately as tracts and in various collections.[91]

In these Finney argued that Christians ought not rest in the experience of that peace from God which comes through regeneration but should persevere in believing prayer until they are endued with that power from God for the work of evangelism which comes through the Baptism in the Holy Spirit.

> There is a great difference between the peace and the power of the Holy Spirit in the soul. The disciples were Christians before the day of Pentecost and as such had a measure of the Holy Spirit. They must have had the peace of sins forgiven, and of a justified state, but yet, they had not the enduement of power necessary to the accomplishment of the work assigned them. They had the peace Christ had *given* them but not the power which he had promised.[92]

The great error of many Christians, ministers included, is that "they rest in conversion and do not seek until they obtain this enduement of power from on high." The empowering which the disciples received on the Day of Pentecost included such gifts as the power of a holy life . . . the power of great meekness . . . the power of a loving enthusiasm in proclaiming the gospel . . . the power of a loving and living faith . . . the power of moral courage.

This Baptism of the Spirit also imparted to these disciples the "power of teaching . . . the gift of tongues . . . an increase of power to work miracles . . . the gift of inspiration." However, concerning all of these enduements, Finney wrote

> neither separately, nor all together did they constitute that power from on high which Christ promised and which they manifestly received. That which they manifestly received as the supreme crowning all important means of success was the power to prevail with both God and man, the power to fasten *saving impressions* upon the minds of men.[93]

This power was demonstrated immediately when Peter preached and 3,000 were converted that very day. The power of the apostles' preaching was "God speaking in and through them. It was a power from on high—God in them making a saving impression upon those to whom they spoke."

Finney described in these articles his own experience of this power resulting from the Baptism in the Spirit he received following his conversion.

> I immediately found myself endued with such power from on high that a few words dropped here and there to individuals were the means of their immediate conversion. My words seemed to fasten like barbed arrows in the souls of men. They cut like a sword, they broke the heart like a hammer.[94]

Without this power, Finney found all of his oratorical abilities to be useless.

> Sometimes I would find myself in a great measure, empty of this power. I would go out and visit and find that I made no saving impression . . . . After humbling myself and crying out for help, the power would return upon me with all its freshness. This has been the experience of my life.[95]

This anointing of power for the purpose of winning the lost is for every Christian. Just as "everyone has the great responsibility devolved upon him or her to win as many souls as possible to Christ," so every one must recognize his or her need for this enduement of power. Just as the great commission to "convert the world" applies to all of Christ's followers, so the promise of power from on high is given to all. This Baptism of power is so important, said Finney, that "the want of an enduement of power from on high should be deemed a disqualification for a pastor, a deacon or elder, a Sabbath-school superintendent, a professor in a Christian college, and especially for a professor in a theological seminary."[96]

The interesting thing to note in these articles is Finney's almost exclusive emphasis upon the Baptism as an empowering for evangelistic ministry rather than the means of permanent sanctification. Finney does affirm that this Baptism imparts the "power of a holy life," but first and foremost, he stresses, it imparts the power to "fasten saving impressions" on the minds of sinners. In these articles Finney returned to a theme that was present as early as his *Lectures on the Revival of Religion* and one which he mentioned from time to time, that the Spirit is given not only for our sanctification but also for our usefulness in the world. Apparently Finney had not discarded his views on the Baptism in the Spirit and sanctification. Rather, the old evangelist was seemingly feeling, once again, his original burden; his great concern in these articles was to see the church, and particularly the ministry, equipped with God's power that they might be effective in winning the lost.

•3•

THE BAPTISM IN THE HOLY SPIRIT AS THE
MEANS OF ENTIRE SANCTIFICATION

[handwritten margin note: If we urge people to testify to entire sanctification, why did John Wesley not do so?]

E ARLY IN HIS MINISTRY, Finney declared that he would crawl on his hands and knees all the way to the Atlantic to see a man who was living in an abiding sanctified state.[1] However, sometime later in his *Lectures to Professing Christians* he argued that just such a state, which he described as Christian perfection, was attainable in this life, even though he himself did not confess such an attainment.[2] In fact, Finney is similar to Wesley in that one cannot find an explicit claim to being entirely sanctified in the writings of either. Finney does describe several "fresh baptisms" in the Spirit during the course of his life which brought him into ever-higher levels of Christian experience, as was discussed above. When Finney urges upon ministers the importance of knowing in their own experience what it means to have received permanent sanctification, one must suppose that he believed himself to have this experience.[3] But because of Finney's view of repeated Baptisms, it is difficult to point to any one crisis as the time of his sanctification.

FINNEY'S UNDERSTANDING OF
CHRISTIAN PERFECTIONISM

Regardless of the time of Finney's own experience of this state, it is clear that as early as 1836–1837, when he gave his *Lectures to Professing Christians*, he believed that Christian perfection or entire sanctification was attainable in this life, and from 1840 on, Finney held that the means of attaining this was through the Baptism in the Holy Spirit. Before dealing more thoroughly with the relationship of Spirit Baptism to sanctification in Finney's theology, it is necessary to describe what he meant by Christian perfection or entire sanctification. His understanding of this concept will become clear through an examination of Finney's three areas of argument for its attainability in this life: philosophical/theological, scriptural, and practical.

Philosophical/Theological Arguments

Finney's first and basic philosophical/theological presupposition is that responsibility implies possibility. According to Finney, "That man cannot be under a moral obligation to perform an absolute impossibility is a first truth of reason."[4] Under the moral government of God, the divine commands imply ability. God would not, indeed, could not, in justice, require anything that could not be accomplished. God governs humanity with a moral government rather than physical force. He rules over moral agents who have the freedom and, therefore, the responsibility and accountability to choose that which is right. Further, that which they are required to choose is within their reach. Even if God were to command people to do something impossible, they would not be obligated to obey, Finney argues, for there could be no obligation without possibility of performance.[5]

Moreover, Finney claims, the law of God is relative to the individual. God's command is that you are to "love the Lord thy God with all *thy* heart, *thy* soul, *thy* mind, *thy* strength." This law does not require anything beyond our strength and abilities, but only that all of our abilities, however limited, be devoted supremely to God.[6] Our responsibility, according to Finney, extends only as far as our knowledge of God's will goes. We cannot be responsible for failing to do something we did not know we were to do. Nor are we required to be as holy as we would have been if we had never sinned. We are required only to devote all of our resources supremely to God, as we are, in our present condition.[7] Thus, Finney argues for the possibility of entire and continual obedience to the divine law on the basis of natural ability. Individuals are able to obey God's law perfectly for the demands of the law are within one's ability.

The second basic philosophical premise underlying Finney's understanding of Christian perfection is that the obedience required by God is a matter of the choice of the will and particularly the supreme choice or ultimate intent of the will. Moral obligation cannot apply to one's feelings, as they are involuntary. Moreover, moral character is not an attribute of the multitude of daily executive choices, but rather the ultimate intention which lies behind and provides the direction for all consequent choices. As Finney says, "Moral obligation respects in the strictest sense and directly, the intention only. . . . This is a first truth of reason."[8] While our moral obligation extends to all our thoughts, actions, and feelings indirectly, the ultimate intent remains the basic determinate of character.[9]

According to Finney, then, the state of perfection or holiness, is a matter of one's supreme intent or ultimate choice, the end toward which one's life is directed. All subsequent choices flow from and gain their moral character from this ultimate intent. That ultimate intent may be described as either selfishness or benevolence.

The essence of sin is selfishness. Selfishness is the making of one's own happiness, the supreme end of life, regardless of the consequences to God or others. A proper self-love and desire for one's own happiness is natural and in no way evil. For the sinner, however, self-gratification becomes the supreme end of life.

For the sanctified, on the other hand, the ultimate intent of the will is to live for the good of God and his universe. The sanctified person regards all others in terms of their true worth. This means that he regards God as of supreme and ultimate value, and his fellow man as having equal value to himself. Thus, his ultimate preference, his end in life, the supreme guiding principle of his life is to love God with all his being and his neighbor as himself. This is what the law of God and reason require. Finney sums it all up in the word "benevolence." By benevolence he means good willing, willing the highest good of being for its own sake.[10]

The moral character of any thought, word, or deed is determined by the ultimate intent of the heart from which it flows, either benevolence or selfishness. Outwardly good acts, which fulfill, perhaps, the letter of the law, but which are done out of a selfish motivation, are sinful. On the other hand, failures in outward performance by one whose ultimate intention is benevolence, are not considered sinful, according to Finney.[11]

From the above, one can begin to gain an understanding of what Finney understood to be the perfect holiness required by God and why it is attainable. God demands what we are able to give. He does not require perfect performance, infinite knowledge, or supernatural strength. He does require a perfect heart, that is, that all of our strength and wisdom, however limited, be devoted supremely to love God and humanity as our ultimate intent. Outward performance may fall short, but where an individual's will is benevolent, choosing the highest good of the universe to the best of his or her knowledge and ability, God considers that person perfectly righteous. People have the natural moral ability to choose benevolence as their ultimate end, and therefore, to be perfect before God.

There remains still a third basic philosophical premise on which Finney's view rests—the idea of the unity of moral action.[12] Finney argues that the will can never at the same time be partly benevolent or partly selfish. Either one motive or the other is the ultimate intention at any one moment.

> Selfishness and benevolence consist in supreme, ultimate, and opposite choices or intentions. To suppose, then, that an intention can be both holy and sinful . . . is naturally impossible.[13]

Thus, the goal of the Christian seeking entire or permanent sanctification is to maintain this benevolent heart from moment to moment without returning time and again to selfishness. How the Holy Spirit enables one to do this, we shall explain. But it may be seen from this, and the preceding, how, given his understanding of perfection, Finney believed in its attainment.

Even though Finney argued for the possibility of entire sanctification on the basis of natural human ability, he was well aware of the power of sin, and he did not rest his case upon natural ability alone. Though people may have a natural ability to obey God's commands, there is a moral inability to do so. An individual's selfishness and unwillingness to obey God is so great that he will never repent and never be holy apart from the agency of the Holy Spirit. Finney argues for the natural ability to render perfect obedience to God's law in order to show that individuals are truly responsible and thus accountable before God to offer that obedience. God's commands are not unreasonable. However, the actual means by which selfish people may actually fulfill that which, though they are naturally able to do, they are morally unwilling to do, is a matter not of human ability but of the grace of God. Finney stresses this fact in his *Systematic Theology.*

> The doctrine of entire sanctification utterly abhors the idea of human merit, disclaims and repudiates it as altogether an abomination to God, and to the sanctified soul. This doctrine, as taught in the Bible and as I understand it is as far as possible from conniving in the least degree at the idea of anything naturally good in saints or sinners. It ascribes the whole of salvation and sanctification from first to last, not only until the soul is sanctified, but at every moment while it remains in that state, to the indwelling spirit and influence and grace of Christ.[14]

Thus, Finney's emphasis on "natural ability" does not negate his equal emphasis on human dependence on the Holy Spirit. Finney believed in the universality of sin.[15] In his doctrine of sin, however, he distinguished between physical depravity and moral depravity. Physical depravity refers to the weakened, diseased, fallen state of our bodies and minds. This state, being involuntary, incurs no guilt.

It does become a source of temptation and the occasion to sin and results in the universal moral depravity of the human race. Moral depravity is "a depravity of choice . . . a sinful heart . . . a voluntary committal of will to self-gratification."[16] Sin, though it is universal, remains a matter of each individual's choice.

Humanity's real problem with sin, then, is not inability but unwillingness.[17] The strength of this unwillingness, however, is so great that no sinner will repent and no believer will persevere in holiness without the grace of God. Consequently, Finney urged that the following instructions be given to new believers.

> Young converts must be made acquainted with the nature and degree of their spiritual wants and dependence. They should be made to see and feel that their "cannot" is their "will not," in other words, that their want of stability of disposition to do the will of God is the only difficulty in the way. But that this instability of disposition is so great, that they are as really dependent upon the influence of divine grace as if obedience to them were naturally impossible.[18]

In this way Finney sought to present a theology in which people were totally and fully responsible for their own sinfulness and yet completely and utterly dependent on God's grace and his Spirit for salvation from sin. The question of the attainment of entire sanctification in this life becomes then a biblical question. This question is, "does God promise within Scripture the grace needed, not only to turn a man from selfishness to benevolence, but also to keep him in that state without wavering?" Finney's answer is a resounding yea and amen.

Scriptural Arguments

Finney's scriptural argument for the possibility of attaining entire sanctification revolves around the divine commands and promises. First, the very command to "be ye perfect" and other similar statements imply the possibility of their fulfillment, for God does not demand impossibilities. Second, and more importantly, the Bible clearly and abundantly promises to believers sufficient divine grace for their entire permanent sanctification. Some of the key Scripture promises to which Finney pointed were Deut. 30:6, Jer. 31:31–34; 32:40, Ezek. 36:25–27.[19]

We have already shown that Finney saw these promises associated with the new covenant in Jeremiah and Ezekiel as blessings for Christians to appropriate now through the Baptism in the Holy Spirit. Finney found entire sanctification promised in the New Testament as well. Paul's prayer for the sanctification of the Thessalonian Christians, "And the very God of peace sanctify you wholly, and I pray your whole spirit and soul and body be preserved blameless unto the coming of our Lord Jesus," was followed by the express promise that "Faithful is he that calleth you, who also will do it."[20]

Finney stressed that the promises are equal to the commands. The new covenant is the fulfillment of all that was required by the old. If the old covenant required perfect and perpetual obedience to God's law, then the new covenant promises sufficient divine grace and help to produce this perfect and perpetual obedience in the life of the believer. This is especially evident, says Finney, when the language of the command and the promise are identical. For example, whatever is commanded in Deut. 10:12:

> What doth the Lord thy God require of thee but to fear the Lord thy God, to walk in all his ways, and to love him, and to serve the Lord thy God with all thy heart, and with all thy soul,

is surely promised in Deut. 30:6: "The Lord thy God will circumcise thine heart . . . to love the Lord thy God with all thine heart and with all thy soul."[21] Finney emphasizes that the promises are important to the believer for

> We never keep the commandments, only as we take hold of the promises. By this I mean that grace alone enables us from the heart to obey the commands of God.[22]

The argument that entire sanctification is attainable in this life does not rest on the question of whether it has ever been actually attained, but it is an encouragement to believers to know that others have attained it. For this reason, Finney argues that the Apostle Paul had clearly attained such a state.[23]

Practical Arguments

In addition to the philosophical and scriptural arguments described thus far, there was a practical basis for Finney's emphasis on the possibility of entire sanctification in this life. Finney's biographer, G. F. Wright, claimed that Finney's real aim in the doctrine was practical. He wanted to lead Christian people into a higher experience and to elevate the general standard of holiness in the church. To do this, the goal toward which Christians are called to strive must be presented as attainable. As Finney stated it, if believers expect to live in sin then they will definitely go on in sin. The people in the church are discouraged from striving after holiness, when the possibility of its attainment is denied.[24]

Finney compared the doctrine of entire sanctification to the principle of "total abstinence" adopted by the Temperance movement of his day. Just as those reformers found that the only means of success was to insist on total abstinence, so Christians must adopt the principle of "total abstinence from sin" in order to avoid being "swept away by sin." Ministers must call upon the church to turn from all sin and present God's grace as sufficient for them to do so.[25]

A final practical argument offered by Finney to the prevalently post-millennial evangelicals of his day was that the millennium would not come if the church failed to teach and appropriate God's promises for entire sanctification in this life.[26]

FINNEY AND SANCTIFICATION

Sanctification and Regeneration

Given these philosophical, scriptural and practical agruments, one can understand how Finney could present entire and permanent sanctification as an attainable state. He defined sanctification as entire consecration to God or "nothing more nor less than entire obedience to the moral law."[27]

This state is entered into through regeneration, which Scripture presents as "a radical change of character, . . . a conversion or turning to God."[28] Regeneration is basically a change of heart. The heart, when used in this connection in Scripture

> is represented not only as the source or fountain of good and evil but as being either good or evil in itself as constituting the character of man. . . .

The heart then

> can be nothing else than the supreme ultimate intention of the soul. . . . A selfish ultimate choice is, therefore, a wicked heart out of which flows every evil and a benevolent ultimate choice is a good heart, out of which flows every good and commendable deed.[29]

Regeneration, then, according to Finney, consists of the following change:

> A change in the attitude of the will or a change in its ultimate choice, intention, or preference; a change from selfishness to benevolence; from choosing self-gratification as the supreme and ultimate end in life to the supreme and ultimate choice of the highest well-being of God and the

universe; from a state of entire consecration to self-interest, self-indulgence, self-gratification for its own sake or as an end, and as the supreme end of life, to a state of entire consecration to God, and to the interests of his kingdom as the supreme and ultimate end of life.[30]

This change is effected through the truths of the gospel as they are pressed upon the consciousness of the sinner by the Holy Spirit and he turns from his selfishness to God. The change thus brought about implies "an entire change of moral character, that is a change from entire sinfulness to entire holiness."[31] Given Finney's philosophical views, one can see how this follows. As a result, there is no sin left in the regenerate heart.

> When the Scriptures require us to grow in grace and in the knowledge of the Lord Jesus, this does not imply that there is yet sin remaining in the regenerate heart which we are to put away only by degrees. But the spirit of the requirement must be that we should acquire as much knowledge as we can of our moral relations and continue to conform to all truth as fast as we know it.[32]

The Need for a Subsequent Work of the Spirit

Regeneration, then, results in the full and complete sanctification of the believer. Where is the need for a subsequent work of the Spirit? What does Finney mean when he refers to entire sanctification as something more than regeneration? Finney explains that by "entire sanctification" or "Christian perfection" he means "permanent sanctification" and he often uses the latter phrase. The regenerate person is fully sanctified—for the moment. However, after regeneration, Christians find themselves falling back into sin and needing to do again their "first works" and return to Christ. In that sense, they are not yet entirely sanctified. Partial as opposed to entire sanctification refers to that "state of mind in which the soul sometimes acts selfishly and at other times benevolently."[33] That sanctification which Christians are to seek is a

> state of being settled, established in faith, rooted and grounded in love, being so confirmed in the faith and obedience of the gospel as to hold on in the way steadfastly, unmovably, always abounding in the work of the Lord.[34]

Entire sanctification refers to a state of "entire and *continued* obedience to the law of God."[35] Finney describes this distinction in one place by presenting regeneration as an "act" of sanctification and "entire sanctification" as an abiding "state" which the regenerate believer must attain.[36]

To understand why there is a need for a subsequent work of the Spirit, as well as how this work establishes the believer in a life of permanent sanctification, one must be aware of Finney's psychology. His understanding of the human psychological make-up forms the background to his discussion of the problems that people need to overcome in order to be sanctified permanently. According to Finney, within human consciousness there reside three faculties: the intellect, the sensibilities (or susceptibilities), and the will. The intellect is the knowing faculty; the sensibility, the feeling faculty; and the will, the choosing faculty.[37] Sanctification respects the will chiefly. The need is to establish the will in permanent consecration to God in an enduring attitude of benevolence. Prior to regeneration, the will is set upon the gratification of self and therefore yields obedience to the sensibilities or feelings rather than the law of God and reason within the intellect. After regeneration, the sensibilities continue to pull upon the will and tempt the Christian to sin. The reason for this is

> the department of our sensibility that is related to objects of time and sense, has received an enormous development and is tremblingly alive to all its correlated objects, while by reason of the blindness of the mind to spiritual objects, it is scarcely developed at all in its relations to them.[38]

When the mind does think upon spiritual realities, which is seldom, it sees them unclearly and only thinks on them. It does not *feel* them. What is needed is a great revelation to the soul of spiritual reality by the Holy Spirit.[39] There needs to be a counter-development of the sensibility in regard to the spiritual realm. This takes place through the revelation of Christ to the soul by the Holy Spirit.

> One great thing that needs to be done to confirm and settle the will in the attitude of entire consecration to God, is to bring about a counter development of the sensibility, so that it will not draw the will away from God. It needs to be mortified or crucified to the world, to objects of time and sense, by so deep, and clear, and powerful a revelation of self to self, and of Christ to the soul, as to awaken and develop all its susceptibilities in their relations to him and to spiritual and divine realities. This can easily be done through and by the Holy Spirit who takes of the things of Christ and shows them to us.[40]

Precisely what the believer needs revealed to him is Christ in all his saving relations. One needs such a revelation of Christ "as to so completely ravish and engross our affections that we would sooner die at once than sin against him."[41] Christ's various relations to the believer "when revealed to the soul and made living realities by the Holy Spirit, tend to kill selfishness and confirm the love of God in the soul."[42]

Sanctification by Christ

Finney presents some sixty-one different relations which Christ sustains to the believer including King, Redeemer, Advocate, Justification, Judge, Propitiation for our sins, Sanctification, Bread of Life, the Vine, True God, Life, and on and on.[43] Finney devotes almost fifty pages of his *Systematic Theology* to extolling the wonderful titles and descriptions of Christ as expressions of the many ways in which he relates to the believers as their Savior from sin. The language is far more devotional in tone than one expects in such a carefully reasoned systematic theology. The roots to Finney's discussion here must lie in the remarkable vision of Christ which captivated his heart on the day of his conversion. As he went on in the Christian faith, Finney apparently continued to experience that the key to victory was found in looking to Christ. He claimed that we sin through ignorance of Christ. We fail to recognize him as the ever-present remedy to our sinfulness. Finney's view of sanctification is decidedly christocentric.

> The soul is saved by Christ himself, not by doctrine, not by the Holy Spirit, not by works of any kind, not by faith, or love, or by anything whatever, but by Christ himself. The Holy Spirit reveals and introduces Christ to the soul and the soul to Christ. He takes of the things of Christ and shows them to us. But he leaves it to Christ to save us.[44]

The Spirit's role in sanctification is definitely subordinated to Christ. "The Holy Spirit sanctifies only by revealing Christ to us as our sanctification."[45] This revelation by the Spirit, however, is absolutely essential. Christ is our sanctification, but, only as he is revealed by the Holy Spirit.[46]

This revelation by the Spirit, of course, is not something extrabiblical. All of the relations Finney describes are taken from Scripture. However, these biblical statements must be made "living realities" by the Holy Spirit. The believer "must have the Bible made a personal revelation of God to his own soul. It must become his own book. He must know Christ for himself."[47]

This revelation of Christ by the Spirit must be appropriated by faith. In the time of temptation, the Spirit will reveal Christ as Savior from sin, and the soul must embrace him and appropriate him.[48] Sanctification comes through putting on Christ by faith, as he is revealed by the Holy Spirit. In this way, the Holy Spirit unites the believer to Christ. This union is not merely "an imagination, a mysticism, a notion, a dream. It must be a living, personal, real entering into a personal and living union with Christ."[49]

Finney is careful to assert that it is not necessary for the believer seeking sanctification first to perceive Christ in all the relations he describes before he can be sanctified. Rather, the Spirit reveals Christ from time to time in various temptations and troubles in that particular relation which is especially suited to the believer's need of the moment. When we are tempted to despair by the enormity of our sin, we need a revelation of Christ as our justification.

In light of the "great subtlety and sagacity" of our spiritual foes, we need a revelation of Christ as our wisdom. The discouraging thought of the number and strength of these spiritual adversaries requires as its antidote a revelation of Christ to the soul as "mighty God, as its strong tower, its hiding place." When our soul is oppressed with the awareness of the infinite distance between us sinners and the holy God, we need to know Christ as our righteousness and our mediator. A revelation of Christ as shepherd and keeper encourages the believer who "trembles" at his "constant exposedness to besetments on every side." Our own emptiness or the total lack of life, power, and spirituality within ourselves is answered by the revelation of Christ as the true vine and the fountain of the water of life.[50]

Sanctification by the Holy Spirit

What believers need, so that Christ will be revealed in such ways and thereby keep them in a state of entire sanctification, is simply to receive the Holy Spirit:

> The thing immediately and directly required is to receive the Holy Spirit by faith to be our teacher and guide, to take of Christ's and show it to us.[51]

Here we find the connection between Finney's discussion of sanctification in his *Systematic Theology* and his discussions elsewhere in which he stresses the Baptism in the Holy Spirit. The Baptism in the Spirit is the prerequisite to that union with Christ which keeps the soul in a state of sanctification. The revelations of Christ in his various relations to the believer are the results of the Baptism in the Spirit. Once the believer has received the Holy Spirit,

> the Holy Spirit, if He is not quenched and resisted, will surely reveal Christ in all his relations in due time so that in every temptation, a way of escape will be open, so that we shall bear it.[52]

The unity between Finney's christocentric teaching on sanctification in his *Systematic Theology* and the more pneumatological teachings in other writings is illustrated in the tract "How to Win Souls," in which Finney stresses that the soul-winner must not rest short of securing the permanent sanctification of his converts through the Baptism in the Spirit. In this tract, as in his *Systematic Theology*, sanctification is presented as a state of permanent consecration to God. The great obstacle to be overcome is the force of the desires of the flesh, or the mind, what Finney refers to in his *Systematic Theology* as the sensibility. He presents the "baptism or sealing of the Holy Spirit" as that which "subdues the power of the desires, and strengthens and confirms the will in resisting the impulse of desire, and in abiding permanently in a state of making the whole being an offering to God." The christological emphasis is present as well, for this experience is also described as receiving "Christ in His fullness into your hearts" and accepting him as "your wisdom, righteousness, sanctification, and redemption."[53]

Thus, the Baptism in the Spirit, for Finney, was the reception of the Spirit as guide and teacher, especially as the one who reveals Christ in such a way as to free the believer from the pull of temptation arising from within and to unite him or her in a conscious experiential union with Christ. Finney emphasized that the Baptism in the Spirit did not effect some change in the believer's nature or impart sanctification as some deposit that rendered subsequent dependence on Christ unnecessary. Rather, the Holy Spirit brought the Christian into that place of union with Christ in which he abides in the believer and the believer in him. Christ then reigns over the soul and by his continual presence and influence keeps it in a state of continual obedience.[54]

Finney's view of the sanctifying work of the Spirit has been criticized for limiting the Spirit's ministry to giving knowledge only.[55] However, the knowledge the Spirit imparts goes beyond mere intellectual knowledge, a fact clearly recognized by Cafone in his study of Finney's pneumatology. He says of Finney's view:

> The Spirit is primarily the Teacher, but the knowledge he imparts is salvific knowledge because it reaches deeply into the person of man rather than residing solely in his intellect. . . . The Holy Spirit is the Revealer, then, in the sense that he is the giver of experience.[56]

This revelation of Christ through the Baptism in the Holy Spirit is usually subsequent to conversion in the life of the believer. New converts enter the Christian life with too little knowledge of themselves and of Christ. They seek to sanctify themselves through "resolutions."

They fail to see that sanctification is by faith. This is true, not only of new converts, Finney claimed, but most of the church. Only after failing again and again does the Christian come to the point at which the Holy Spirit may reveal to the believer his complete helplessness. Then, the believer is prepared for that revelation of Christ as the remedy to his sins. At that point, the believer is ready to ask God for a greater anointing of the Holy Spirit that he may know Christ as his sanctification.[57] Thus, believers are not permanently sanctified at conversion, but subsequently, through the Baptism in the Holy Spirit.

•4•

THE BAPTISM IN THE HOLY SPIRIT

IN RELATION TO MINISTRY, PRAYER, AND

CHRISTIAN EXPERIENCE

THE BAPTISM IN THE HOLY SPIRIT AS AN
ENDUEMENT OF POWER FOR MINISTRY

AS WE HAVE SEEN IN OUR SURVEY of Finney's writings, he saw the Baptism in the Holy Spirit not only as the means of entire sanctification, but also as an enduement of power for ministry. This Baptism gives the believer "power to prevail with God and man."[1] Power to prevail with man refers to empowered preaching, "the power to fasten saving impressions upon the minds of men,"[2] that is, preaching which has the power to secure the conviction and conversion of its listeners. Power to prevail with God, on the other hand, refers to power in prayer. Finney always used the phrase "to prevail with God" in reference to prayer.[3] The passage of Scripture from which Finney took this phrase is the account of Jacob's successful struggle in prayer in which he received God's blessing (Gen. 32:28). Finney believed that the Holy Spirit enables the Christian to pray in such a way that his prayers are answered. We will discuss, first, Finney's understanding of the Baptism as an anointing for preaching with divine power to prevail with people, and second, his view of this experience as receiving "the Spirit of Prayer," which affords believers power to prevail with God. We shall see in both cases that his power comes from the Spirit uniting the believer to Christ.

Power in Preaching

For Finney the essential ingredient for ministerial success, which he emphasized with great force in several writings, was the "enduement of power from on high" through the Baptism of the Holy Spirit.[4] Finney's own experience bore this out. As a result of the "overwhelming baptisms of the Holy Ghost" following his conversion, Finney claimed, "I immediately found myself endued with such power from on high that a few words dropped here and there to individuals were the means of their immediate conversion."[5] Finney claimed that he experienced this power throughout his life. Whenever he found himself unsuccessful in securing conversions, he would humble himself and cry out to God until this power returned.[6]

Finney's preaching was powerful and his evangelism was successful. One writer claimed that

> during the year 1857–58 over a hundred thousand persons were led to Christ as the direct or indirect result of Finney's labours while five hundred thousand persons professed conversion to Christ in the great revival which began in his meetings. . . . It was found by actual research that over eighty-five in every hundred persons professing conversion to Christ in Finney's meetings remained true to God.[7]

While these figures may be somewhat exaggerated and are impossible to verify, they illustrate the high evaluation often given of Finney's power as an evangelistic preacher, a power he attributed to the anointing of the Holy Spirit.

Finney's stress upon the importance of the Baptism in the Spirit for effective ministry was rooted, not only in his personal experience, but also in his understanding of conversion. According to Finney, there are several agencies involved in conversion. At the outset, we must note that conversion and regeneration are synonymous. Regeneration is not a divine action preceding the actual turning or conversion of the sinner. Rather, both terms refer to the moral transformation of the sinner in which both the divine and human agents are simultaneously active.[8] Regeneration involves the Holy Spirit, the subject of regeneration, and other human agents such as preachers of the gospel. First and foremost is the Holy Spirit. Jesus said that one must be "born of the Spirit" (John 3:6). Second, the sinner himself is not passive, but actively involved, for regeneration consists in his change of ultimate choice. Third, there are usually other human agents who effect the sinner's regeneration by persuading him to change. Thus, Paul says to his converts, "I have begotten you through the gospel"; this suggests his active role in their regeneration. The instrumentality used to effect regeneration is the truth, more particularly the truths of the gospel. A person is converted when the Holy Spirit, usually through and along with some Christian, presents the truths of the gospel to the sinner and he or she responds in faith and repentance by turning to Christ.[9]

Finney illustrated these agencies by the analogy of a man about to fall unawares into the deadly waters of Niagara Falls who is saved when another man shouts a warning.[10] The man who was thus saved could attribute his rescue either to the words that he heard (corresponding to the instrumentality of truth), the man who warned him (the preacher of the gospel), or himself, since it was he who stepped back once he was warned (the sinner's own response to the gospel). Finally, the man could attribute the whole of the matter to God, who in his providence had someone there at the right time to warn him. This last part of the analogy falls short, Finney admits. There is much more to God's involvement in regeneration than providence, though God's providence does play an important role in preparing sinners for the gospel and making the gospel available to them. God's role is much more than this, for it is only as the Holy Spirit reveals the truth inwardly and powerfully persuades the sinner to accept that truth that a person is regenerated.

The necessity of the Spirit's agency is due, strictly speaking, not to the sinner's inability, for Finney argued for the individual's natural ability to obey God's law. Rather, Finney wrote, "the sinner's dependence upon the Holy Spirit arises entirely out of his own voluntary stubbornness."[11] Because of this "voluntary stubbornness" people will not be saved apart from the powerful inward revelation of the Spirit. The need for the Holy Spirit arises from the fact that sinful humanity shuts its mind to all the motives and considerations which call it away from sin to holiness. The sinner's mind is full of his or her own selfish pursuits and resists as far as possible the demands of reason, conscience, and the Bible.[12] The Holy Spirit, having direct access to the mind and a perfect knowledge of the sinner, can present the truths of the gospel with such "vividness, strength, and power" as to arrest the sinner's attention and gain the consent of his will.[13]

The Holy Spirit's ministry involves more than merely teaching the sinner.

> The work of the Holy Spirit does not consist in merely giving instruction but in compelling him (the sinner) to consider truths which he already knows—to think upon his ways and turn to the Lord. He urges upon his attention and consideration those motives which he hates to consider and feel the weight of.[14]

The Spirit carries on "debates and strivings with the mind" of the sinner.[15] The exact manner of this communication is a mystery. The sinner is not aware of the Spirit himself, but rather is conscious of perceiving and feeling the truth and finding his attention drawn to the consideration of spiritual things. The truth is known not only intellectually, but its influence is felt in a powerful way. As Finney said, "There is, so to speak, a sort of heat, a warmth and vitality attending the truth when enforced by the Spirit."[16] However, it is a great mistake, claimed Finney, for sinners to expect to feel some physical influence before they may be saved. The Spirit's work is one of divine moral persuasion.[17]

Finney, along with the other New School theologians was criticized for presenting the Spirit's work as only an "influence." To answer such criticisms we must point out why Finney described the work of the Spirit in this way. He wanted to emphasize that personal sinfulness and the consequent necessity of dependence on the Holy Spirit were caused by one's own stubborn will and not by any deficiency in natural ability. The Spirit's work is not to supply some deficiency in one's ability. That would imply that the individual disobeys God from his lack of natural ability and is therefore not responsible.[18] God's giving of the Spirit to enable the individual to do what was otherwise physically impossible would simply be a matter of justice on God's part, not grace, according to Finney.[19] By describing the Spirit's work in terms of influence, Finney sought to show the individual's own responsibility for his sin and God's grace and love in persuading sinners to repent and be sanctified. Further, by describing the work of the Spirit in this way, Finney could stress the Christian's continual reliance on the Holy Spirit. The Spirit does not somehow effect some change in a human nature or physical make-up through regeneration or the Baptism in the Spirit. If that were true, the Christian could then live in holiness in his own strength without further need for the Holy Spirit.[20] Rather, Finney would say, the Spirit sanctifies by changing the will through divine influence and maintaining the will in obedience through continuing that divine influence. Thus, Finney could show human activity in the process of sanctification and allow the possibility of resisting the Spirit.[21] This view of the Spirit's work also shows the place of the minister of the gospel as a co-worker with God, who presents the truth and persuades the sinner to repent along with and as instrument of the Holy Spirit.[22]

From Finney's understanding of the agencies in conversion and the particular manner of the Spirit's work, one can begin to see the importance of Spirit-anointed preaching. The Spirit's agency in conversion is indispensable. The normal means through which the Holy Spirit influences the sinner is through the agency of Christians preaching the gospel. Preachers are to preach persuasively the truths of the gospel with reasonable arguments and with great earnestness and directness as God's co-workers.[23] To be successsful, this preaching must be "God speaking in and through them."[24]

Thus, the first thing to be done by those who believe they have a call from God to the ministry is to pray for the Baptism in the Spirit, that divine anointing of power from on high.[25] This experience is not for ministers alone, however. Just as the Great Commission, the task of converting the world, as Finney put it, is given to all Christians, even so, the promise of power to fulfill that task is given to all Christians in every age and place. No Christian should rest in conversion and the experience of God's peace and not seek the Baptism in the Spirit that brings God's power. This enduement of power should be a requirement for any spiritual office. Not only pastors, but elders, deacons, Sunday School superintendents, and seminary and college professors ought not be accepted if they lack this power. One of the great failures of the theological seminaries, Finney held, was their lack of emphasis on the necessity of the Baptism in the Spirit as essential to pastoral preparation.[26]

Finney's understanding of the nature of the Spirit's anointing is illustrated by his approach to preaching. Contrary to the common practice of the day, Finney preached extemporaneously. He would pray and look to the Holy Spirit to "suggest a text and to open up the whole subject to my mind."[27] The Spirit would make such powerful impressions upon his mind, Finney said, that he would even tremble. Finney regarded the message he preached as not his own but as coming "from the Holy Spirit in me." He claimed that he preached from "inspiration" but not an inspiration unique to him. Finney believed that

> all ministers, called by Christ to preach the gospel, ought to be, and may be, in such a sense inspired, as to "preach the gospel with the Holy Ghost sent down from heaven."[28]

Finney gave the following advice to the preachers:

> Always present the subject which the Holy Spirit lays upon your heart for the occasion. Seize the points presented by the Holy Spirit to your own mind, and present them with the greatest possible directness to your congregation. Be full of prayer whenever you attempt to preach and go from your closet to the pulpit with the inward groanings of the Spirit pressing for utterance at your lips. Get your mind fully endowed with your subject, so that it will press for an utterance, then open your mouth and let it forth like a torrent.[29]

While not explicitly stated by Finney, it seems that the source of this power, similar to sanctification, is the union with Christ effected by the Holy Spirit. Through the anointing of the Spirit, the preacher is united with Christ in such a way that he does not merely preach about Christ—Christ himself speaks through him. This is a fulfillment of Christ's promise, given along with the Great Commission in Matthew, when he said, "Lo, I am with you always even unto the end of the world," as well as his promise that the Holy Spirit "shall take of mine and show it unto you."[30] When the preacher's message originates from the Holy Spirit, there is such a union between the preacher and God that the people will say of such preachers "God is in them of a truth."[31] The Spirit inspires the preacher's words and even his feelings, so that in his preaching it is as if Christ himself were addressing the sinner through the sermon.[32] The minister of the gospel must have this unity with Christ. Finney claimed that the inefficiency of the Christian ministry was due to a lack of communion with God, a lack of sympathy and fellowship with him.[33] Ministers needed "a deep sympathy and fellowship between the Holy Ghost and us" in which

> we feel as He does, and that He feels as we do; that we have a common object in view; that we are influenced by the same motives, interested in the same objects, employed in the same labors.[34]

In a sermon on "The Great Harvest," Finney urged that in order to win souls,

> you must have so much of the love of God—a love like God's love for sinners—in your soul, that you are ready for any sacrifice or any labor. You need to feel as God feels.[35]

This union is secured through the "gift of the Holy Spirit."[36] The preacher who is baptized with the Holy Spirit, who has this anointing from God, preaches with great power because his text, message, and words originate from God. His sermons, moreover, are full of feeling as his heart is full of God's love for sinners, and thus that love of God is conveyed to the sinner through the preacher.

POWER IN PRAYER

Sinners are not won through preaching alone, however, but through preaching and prayer, particularly Spirit-inspired prayer. The Baptism in the Spirit is the key to empowered prayer. "The Spirit in the hearts of saints," Finney said, "is pre-eminently a Spirit of prayer."[37] One of the consequences of being filled with the Holy Spirit is that one will be useful to God, even if he is an invalid, for he will have power in prayer.[38] Finney refers to the Holy Spirit as "the Spirit of Prayer."[39] In His *Revival Lectures*, "having the Spirit of Prayer" is synonymous with "being filled with the Spirit." Both phrases are early expressions of what Finney later referred to as the Baptism in the Holy Spirit.

Commenting on Rom. 8:26–27, Finney described the various ways in which the Holy Spirit helps the believer intercede. He aids the Christian's prayer life in the following ways: The Spirit enlightens the mind to perceive spiritual realities. This revelation of the Spirit awakens the sensibilities so that the praying Christian deeply feels the concerns of God's heart. The Spirit guides the interceding Christian in understanding and applying the promises of Scripture in prayer. Further, the Spirit directs the Christian to pray for specific individuals, places, or needs. The Spirit gives the praying Christian insight into God's providence and lets him know that the time is ripe for revival, that he may pray with confidence.[40]

Unlike the Pentecostal view of speaking in tongues, Finney claimed that the Holy Spirit did not direct the Christian's prayers by immediately suggesting words to his mind or by guiding his language. However, similar to that view, Finney did believe that Spirit-inspired prayer allowed the believer to transcend the limits of human language. He based his view on a very literal interpretation and application of the passage in Romans, "the Spirit maketh intercession with groanings that cannot be uttered." Finney understood this to mean

> that the Spirit excites desires too great to be uttered except by groans. Something that language cannot utter—making the soul too full to utter its feelings by words, where the person can only groan them out to God who understands the language of the heart.[41]

Not only in his earlier writings, but in an article as late as 1851, Finney referred to such groanings in the Spirit. He referred to them as "travailing in birth for souls" and marveled at the "almost unutterable agony of mind" Christians experienced in such deep intercession.[42]

As one would expect, Finney had such experiences in his own prayer life. One of his first such experiences is described in his memoirs. This experience grew out of Finney's concern for an unconverted woman who was sick to the point of death. As Finney relates:

> The burden was so great that I left the house almost immediately and went up to the meeting house to pray for her. There I struggled, but could not say much. I could only groan with groanings loud and deep. . . . For a long time I tried to get my prayer before the Lord; but somehow words could not express it. I could only groan and weep without being able to express what I wanted in words. . . . (Finally) I obtained the assurance in my own mind that the woman would not die, and indeed that she would never die in her sins.[43]

Needless to say, the woman did not die and she was converted.

The secret of the Spirit-inspired prayer is that in such prayer believers are united with God, for their prayers are originated and energized by the Spirit of God within them, even to the point of inarticulate groanings. These are prayers from God to God. In the process, the believer experiences a deep union with Christ in his love for sinners.

> It is as if Christ came and poured the overflowing of his own benevolent heart into His people and led them to sympathize and co-operate with Him as they never do in any other way. They feel just as Christ feels, so full of compassion for sinners, that they cannot contain themselves.[44]

These feelings, which the Christian expresses in his prayers, spoken or simply groaned out to God, "strongly illustrate the strength of God's feelings. They are like the real feelings of God for impenitent sinners."[45] Finney rejected the traditional doctrine of God's impassibility. The biblical descriptions of God's feelings are not mere accommodations to human understanding but descriptions of the real emotions of God's heart. Finney urged Christians to "conceive of God as He really is, a being who not only knows but pities and deeply yearns over you with all the feelings of a heart of infinite sensibility."[46] Thus, in prayer, the believer could share in God's own feelings for lost sinners.

Since such Spirit-inspired prayer expresses God's own desires, God will surely answer:

> When we are conscious of sympathizing with God Himself, we may know that God will answer our prayers. There never was a prayer made in this state of sympathy with God which He failed to answer. God cannot fail to answer such a prayer without denying Himself. The soul, being in sympathy with God, feels as God feels, so that for God to deny its prayers, is to deny His own feelings, and refuse to do the very thing He himself desires. Since God cannot do this, he cannot fail of hearing the prayer that is in sympathy with his own heart.[47]

Such prayer is "Spirit-inspired prayer" or "prayer in the Spirit." God may not answer exactly to the letter, but he will always answer the spirit of these requests.[48]

This union with God through the Holy Spirit is the most important condition of answered prayer, according to Finney, "All the hindrances to prayer may be summed up in one, which is one of the greatest, if not the greatest, of difficulties—I refer to a want of sympathy with God."[49] This "sympathy" or union with God is not only a matter of sharing God's feelings, but includes as well a union of will. One must have a sincere desire to see God's kingdom established on the earth,

his will done in the world. The praying Christian must be supremely
devoted to the task of saving souls, as God is, in order to have his
prayers answered.[50]

The means of obtaining the Spirit's influence in prayer, Finney
claimed, was simply to ask for it, pointing to Jesus' promise of the
Holy Spirit to those who ask in Luke 11:13. In order to receive the
"Spirit of Prayer," Finney says, "Persevere in prayer and effort til you
obtain the blessing of the Spirit of God to dwell in you."[51]

In regard to prayer, Finney gave excellent advice for distinguishing
the influences of the Holy Spirit. Any concern that is felt for sinners,
any drawing of the mind to their needs, any benevolent desires and
feelings arising within the heart of the believer are clearly the results
of the Spirit's influence and are to be cherished and given expression
through prayer. Furthermore, all supposed impressions of the Spirit
are to be judged in light of biblical revelation. As Finney said,
"Compare your desires with the spirit and temper of religion as
described in the Bible." The Holy Spirit does not merely impart ideas
or suggestions but rather moves upon the believer's heart, imparting
divine love.[52]

THE BAPTISM IN THE HOLY SPIRIT AS
EXPERIENTIAL UNION WITH CHRIST

It is at first difficult to relate Finney's two emphases which I have
described. Is the Baptism in the Spirit sanctification, empowering, or
both? It is clear from the preceding material that Finney believed in
both. In his articles on "Power From On High," Finney seemed to place
the priority upon the empowering for ministry. He claimed that one
could be free from all forms of sin and not yet have this blessing.
However, while the power imparted through this Baptism was chiefly
the power to "fasten saving impressions upon the minds of men,"
it did include as well, "the power of a holy life."[53] So, even there the
emphasis on sanctification is not absent.

The underlying unity to both of Finney's emphases, as has already
been suggested and illustrated, is that both the power for preaching
and prayer and the power to overcome sin and persevere in obedience
are realized through the Spirit uniting the believer to Christ
experientially. In sanctification, the power of temptation over the
sensibility is broken by the Spirit's revelation of Christ as our Savior
dwelling within and reigning over the soul. In ministry, preaching is
empowered as one is united to Christ by the Spirit and enabled to

preach with his wisdom, his love, even his feeling for the lost, whereby the preacher's sermon becomes like the very voice of God. In prayer, too, the Spirit unites the believer to Christ so that the Christian's deeply felt, Spirit-inspired prayers are the expression of the desires of God's own heart as he prays through his people by the Spirit. This prayer is powerful, for God cannot fail to answer those prayers which he himself has inspired. Thus, the Baptism in the Spirit sanctifies and empowers through bringing the Christian into a deeper experience of union with Christ.

This concept grew out of Finney's own experience. For example, following his "fresh baptism of the Spirit" in the winter of 1843–1844, Finney claimed, "At this time it seemed as if my soul was wedded to Christ in a sense in which I had never had any thought or conception of before. The language of the Song of Solomon was as natural to me as my breath."[54] In his discussion of the "Essential Elements of Christian Experience," Finney said that the Baptism in the Spirit could be described as an "eating the flesh and drinking the blood of the Lord Jesus, so really does the soul seem to live on Christ."[55]

In the sermon "On Prayer for the Holy Spirit," Finney speaks of this experience as the means of union with God. Finney wrote that "the gift of the Holy Spirit comprehends all that we need spiritually" for it "secures to us that union with God which is eternal life."[56] The goal of God's dealings with humanity and the object of the Spirit's work is to effect this union:

> The gospel scheme was purposed for the end of accomplishing this complete union and sympathy between our souls and God, so that the soul should enjoy God's own peace and should be in the utmost harmony with its maker and Father. Hence it is the great business of the Spirit to bring about this state.[57]

Finney's emphasis on the Holy Spirit's ministry of uniting the believer to God, or more specifically, to Christ, is similar to Calvin's view.[58] Finney differs, however, in his stress upon the experiential nature of this union. For Finney, "Religion is an experience. It is a consciousness," and thus union with Christ must be a conscious experience.[59]

While the Spirit of Christ dwells within every believer, one must know Christ living within experientially through the Baptism in the Spirit in order to be established in the life of sanctification and empowered for ministry:

> We not only need the real presence of Christ within us, but we need his manifested

presence to sustain us in hours of conflict. . . . To know Christ after the flesh, or merely historically as an outward savior is of no spiritual avail. We must know him as an inward Savior, as Jesus risen and reigning in us, as having arisen and established his throne in our hearts, and as having written and established the authority of his love there.[60] (italics mine)

This conscious union with Christ begins at the very moment of initial faith. However, because of a limited knowledge of Christ, beginning faith may be weak and this consciousness dim. When this faith is stronger, though,

it lets a current of the divine love into our souls so strong that it seems to permeate both soul and body. We then know in consciousness what it is to have Christ's Spirit within us as a power to save us from sin and stay up our feet in the path of loving obedience.[61]

That greater consciousness of Christ's presence within is the result of the Baptism in the Spirit. In the sermon, "On Prayer for the Holy Spirit," Finney presents the results of being filled with the Spirit as "a deep union with God . . . a consciousness of God in the soul . . . (a certain knowledge) that God's Spirit is within you. . . . His presence becomes a conscious reality."[62]

Finney presented the Holy Spirit as the divine teacher who "takes of the things of Christ and shows them to us (John 16:14)."[63] That knowledge is not merely intellectual but experiential. As Cafone remarks in the statement previously quoted, "the Holy Spirit is the Revealer, then, in the sense that he is the giver of experience." Then he adds, "It is a personal religious experience which lies at the heart of Finney's brand of Christianity."[64] Therein lies the importance of the Baptism in the Spirit for Finney's view of the Christian life. It is through receiving the Holy Spirit in his fullness that the believer's union with Christ becomes a conscious experiential reality and therefore, a sanctifying and empowering reality.

In this union with Christ, into which the Holy Spirit brings the believer, the Christian comes to know experientially the infinite measure of God's grace and the fullness of salvation in Christ. In describing this state Finney verges on the mystical:

When drawn into this form of communion with the Holy Spirit, whose business is to take of the things of Christ and show them to us, (the soul) sees in him such infinite fullness and security, such a world of promises, so vast in their meaning, so true, so infinitely certain in their fulfillment that they are all yea and amen in Christ Jesus. The soul feels at such times that it is indeed complete in Him, that He is a perfect Righteousness, a perfect Sanctification, a perfect Redemption; that his grace and fullness are large enough to swallow up all thought, all finite conception; that the sins of all mankind might be merged in the ocean of his grace; that all the temptations and wants and woes of man might all be swallowed up in the boundless ocean of his love and grace and would all be only as a pebble in the midst of the great Pacific Ocean.[65].

•5•

THE SUBSEQUENCE OF THE BAPTISM
IN THE HOLY SPIRIT

ONE OF THE MOST CONTROVERSIAL ASPECTS of Finney's doctrine of the Baptism in the Spirit is his view that this experience is distinct from and subsequent to regeneration. Two recent scholarly works are quite critical of this view as it is represented today in the Holiness and Pentecostal movements.[1] As this continues to be a divisive issue regarding the Baptism in the Spirit, and since Finney has played such an important role in the rise of this belief, it might prove helpful to consider Finney's own arguments for the subsequence of this experience. His arguments vary somewhat depending on whether he is considering the Baptism as an anointing for ministry or as the means to permanent sanctification.

If considered in regard to its effect on the believer's ministry, Finney's argument rests on the distinction between conversion, commission, and anointing. These distinctions are illustrated in the experiences of the apostles. The apostles, Finney says, were Christians before the Day of Pentecost. However, it was only just prior to his ascension that Jesus gave them their commission to carry the gospel throughout the world. With that commission came the promise of the divine power necessary for its fulfillment which they received on the Day of Pentecost.[2]

As it was with the apostles, so it continues to be—conversion, commission, and anointing are distinct experiences in the Christian life. Conversion is "a personal transaction between the soul and Christ relating to its own salvation," whereas commission is "the soul's acceptance of the service in which Christ proposes to employ it." With the commission comes "the admonition and the promise" that those who wait upon the Lord in faith shall receive power through the Baptism in the Spirit.[3] Finney urged young preachers to be sure that they were truly converted, called, and anointed before embarking upon their ministries. He told them:

> Do not confound a call to the ministry with an anointing to the work. . . .
> Remember, conviction is one thing. Regeneration is still another. A call
> to the ministry is distinct from both and a special anointing to the work
> of which I am speaking is another and a gift distinct and by itself.[4]

While this is especially true for preachers, it is also true for all
believers. The Great Commission, as well as the promise of power
to fulfill that commission, is given to every believer. "The great want
of the Church at present is, first, the realizing conviction that this
commission to convert the world is given to each of Christ's disciples
as his life-work . . . the second great want is a realizing conviction
of the necessity of this enduement of power upon every individual
soul."[5] Thus, Finney concluded there is a difference between "the *peace*
and the *power* of the Holy Spirit in the soul." One may be a Christian,
having "a measure of the Holy Spirit . . . the peace of sins forgiven
and of a justified state," but not yet be endued with power from on
high, anointed for the work of the ministry through the Baptism in
the Holy Spirit.[6]

When viewing the Baptism in the Spirit as the means of establishing
the believer in a life of permanent sanctification, Finney's arguments
for subsequence revolve around his understanding of this Baptism
as the fulfillment of the promises of the new covenant. For Finney,
the new covenant is the "effectual indwelling of the Spirit producing
the very temper required by the law or Old Covenant."[7] Whereas the
old covenant required perfect and perpetual obedience, the new
covenant is "the producing of this perfect and perpetual obedience."[8]
Finney claimed that "the argument in favor of entire sanctification
may be settled to a demonstration by looking at what the old covenant
required and recognizing that as the highest perfection that God
requires of man, and then seeing that this Old Covenant is to be
written in the heart by the Spirit of God."[9]

If the new covenant is to produce entire and permanent
sanctification, as Finney argues, these promises of the new covenant
must include more than regeneration. The Old Testament saints were
regenerated, says Finney, but they did not receive the promises of
the new covenant as is stated in Heb. 11:13, 39–40. "The thing that
Abraham and the Old Testament saints did not receive," Finney
explained, "was that measure of the Holy Spirit which constitutes the
New Covenant and produces the entire sanctification of the soul."[10]
This promised outpouring of the Spirit was referred to by both John
the Baptist and Jesus as the Baptism in the Holy Spirit.[11] Christians
who have not yet experienced such a "measure of the Holy Spirit"

are like the Old Testament saints, who were regenerate but had not received the promised blessings of the new covenant. Such Christians need to "receive this gift of the Holy Ghost through faith."[12] The New Testament teaches that this experience is subsequent to regeneration, quite explicitly for Finney, in Eph. 1:13. There it states that it is "after" (KJV) believing that Christians are sealed with the Holy Spirit of Promise.[13]

One could ask why regeneration is insufficient to ensure the believer's permanent sanctification or why the believer's initial faith fails to secure both regeneration and the Baptism in the Spirit. Finney's explanation was that new believers usually do not have a sufficiently large enough view of Christ and the provisions of the gospel. They trust Christ as their justification, but fail to see that he may be their sanctification as well. Further, new Christians often have to go through the process of failing at all their own efforts to establish themselves in the sanctified life before realizing their desperate and complete dependence upon Christ and the Holy Spirit.[14]

In evaluating Finney's arguments for the subsequence of the Baptism in the Spirit, it can first be pointed out that his appeal to Eph. 1:13 does not necessarily prove his point, for the sealing of the Spirit, referred to there, could be either subsequent to or simultaneous with believing. Either idea is grammatically possible and commentators could be cited on either side.[15]

Second, Finney's view that the Old Testament saints were regenerated is debatable. For many, including those who believe that the Baptism in the Spirit is a distinct and subsequent experience, regeneration itself is also a distinctly new covenant experience.[16] It must be noted however, that for Finney, regeneration is essentially identical with conversion. It is a moral transformation, a move from self-centeredness to God-centeredness as one's ultimate intent. To Finney then, it was obvious that the Old Testament saints who trusted God and obeyed him were regenerate.

While Finney's definition of regeneration may be inadequate and the experience erroneously attributed to those living prior to the coming of the Messiah, his basic argument is still valid. That is, the new covenant promises a much greater experience of the Holy Spirit than most experience at the beginning of their Christian life. Since regeneration is identified with the beginning of the Christian life, the much fuller experience of the Holy Spirit's sanctifying power, prophesied in the Old Testament as a fulfillment of the new covenant and referred to by Jesus and John the Baptist as the Baptism in the

Holy Spirit, must be a distinct and subsequent experience.

Some would counter this argument by affirming that one receives all the blessings of the new covenant at the initial moment of faith in the gospel, even though the actual experience of these blessings may follow subsequently. For Finney, however, the Baptism in the Spirit is experiential by definition. This experiential understanding of Spirit Baptism is the basic idea which underlies all of his arguments for subsequence. Thus, while the Holy Spirit has been given to the church, no believer can be said to have been baptized in the Spirit until he individually appropriates the power of the Spirit in his own experience. Finney wrote that "the promises made to the church as a *body* belong to *individuals* of the Church. The Church is composed of individuals, and the promises are of no avail any further than there is an individual application of them."[17]

Because the Baptism is an experience it is usually subsequent to the believer's conversion. Most believers have to go through struggles before recognizing their need to appropriate the power of the Spirit for their sanctification. Or, if the Baptism is considered as enduement of power, it is usually after conversion that one becomes aware that he or she is now commissioned by Christ to enter into his service. At that point, the believer becomes aware of the need for divine anointing and is prepared to receive the power of the Spirit promised by the Lord. Of course often the failure to receive the Baptism in the Spirit at the beginning of the Christian life is in the teaching of the church, as Finney pointed out. New converts are not aware of the blessing available to them or their responsibility to appropriate this blessing by faith.

This understanding of the Baptism as an experience is often the great division between the two sides in the argument over subsequence, a point noted by Clark Pinnock.[18] Writing as a sympathetic observer of the Charismatic movement, he emphasizes that Baptism in the Spirit, for charismatics, does not refer to a doctrine but an experience. The Baptism in the Spirit for charismatics, is not merely a doctrine to be believed, it is an encounter which must be experienced.

I would argue that the New Testament points to this as a definite experience. How else could the Apostle Paul ask, "Did you receive the Holy Spirit when you believed?" or "Did you receive the Spirit by the works of the Law or by hearing with faith?" (Acts 19:2; Gal. 3:2). How would these questions be answered except by reference to an experience? Even though the Samaritans believed and were baptized, it was clear to observers that the Holy Spirit "had not yet fallen upon any of them" (Acts 8:8). While these converts had experienced what is commonly understood to be the signs of regeneration—repentance, faith in the gospel, and water baptism, there was a further dimension of the Spirit still missing in their experience.

James D. G. Dunn argues against subsequence, yet recognizes the experiential nature of Spirit Baptism. He says, "That the Spirit, and particularly the gift of the Spirit, was a fact of experience in the lives of the earliest Christians has been too obvious to require elaboration."[19] While he rejects a view of the Baptism in the Spirit as a second reception of the Spirit, Dunn does recognize Spirit Baptism as subsequent to the act of repentance and faith, expressed in water baptism. Thus, Dunn has his own view of subsequence. Only he would not say that Baptism in the Spirit is subsequent to becoming a Christian, for one does not become a Christian at the point of initial faith or even at water baptism, but at the point of Baptism in the Spirit.[20] Bruner, on the other hand, in his arguments against subsequence seeks to unite water baptism and Spirit Baptism. "A Spirit-less baptism in water or a water-less baptism in the Spirit are ordinary impossibilities."[21] Even Bruner, however, has a doctrine of subsequence, for this Baptism in water and the Spirit is subsequent to the moment of initial faith.

Finney and his spiritual descendants in the Holiness and Pentecostal movements are criticized as having in their theologies two receptions of the Spirit, one at regeneration, one at Spirit Baptism. This is because they are convinced that Spirit Baptism is subsequent to the moment of initial faith, as Bruner and Dunn would agree. However, they are equally convinced, as are most Evangelicals, that the initial moment of faith and repentance is evidence of the Holy Spirit's regenerating presence. Thus, a believer must have, as Finney says, "a measure of the Spirit" from the moment of initial faith, even though he is not yet "filled with the Spirit." (These kinds of quantitative statements are to be understood in terms of the believer's experience.)

The positive contribution that Bruner and Dunn can make to our understanding of the Baptism in the Holy Spirit is that it is a part of the process of "conversion-initiation" (Dunn's phrase) in the New Testament. Spirit Baptism in the early church was part of a complex of events which formed a whole. As F. F. Bruce says:

> It must be remembered, in New Testament times, repentance and faith, regeneration and conversion, baptism in water, reception of the Holy

Spirit, incorporation into Christ, admission to church fellowship and first communion were all parts of a single complex of events which took place within a very short time and not always in a uniform order. Logically they were distinguishable but in practice they were all bound up with the transition from the old life to the new.[22]

Recognizing this, Charismatic theologian J. Rodman Williams offers the following suggestions:

What is needed, first of all, is an understanding of baptism with the Holy Spirit that views this baptism as an aspect of Christian initiation. That is to say, Spirit Baptism is not an addition to becoming a Christian (which view sets up two categories of Christians) but is the climactic moment of entrance into Christian life. It is not to be identified with redemption (cleansing, forgiveness) but with the gift of God's presence and power. The two, while belonging together in the totality of Christian initiation, often are separated in their actual occurrence. This may be understood from the perspective of Christian initiation as a process involving both forgiveness of sins (redemption) and the gift of the Holy Spirit (cf. Acts 2:38). Thus, it is not proper to speak of Christians and Spirit-baptized Christians but only of persons in process of Christian initiation.

Here two mistaken positions are to be avoided: one that would identify becoming Christian with either the first or second moment, the other that would devalue such moments so that they are viewed as unimportant in the process of becoming Christian.[23]

Finney seemed to approach such a view of Spirit Baptism as a part of Christian initiation in his appeals to ministers to be sure that new converts are baptized in the Holy Spirit.[24]

•6•

CONDITIONS FOR RECEIVING THE
BAPTISM IN THE SPIRIT

IN HIS INVESTIGATION OF the Pentecostal doctrine of the Baptism in the Spirit, F. D. Bruner's primary criticism is that the Pentecostals, following their Holiness predecessors, establish conditions other than faith for receiving God's free gift of the Holy Spirit![1] As in the question of subsequence, since Finney was such an important figure in the rise of these movements, it is interesting to consider his own view of the conditions for receiving the Holy Spirit.

Interestingly, Finney does not stress conditions for receiving the Baptism in the Spirit as much as he emphasizes the availability of this gift for every believer. He claimed that it is "supremely easy to obtain this gift from God."[2] As Jesus pointed out in Luke 11:11–13, speaking about receiving the Holy Spirit, it is "easy for children to get really good things from their father." Finney's emphasis on God's willingness to give the Holy Spirit to his children immediately raised the question of why, then, do so many fail to receive the Baptism in the Spirit. It is in answer to that kind of question that Finney discusses conditions.

One reason why many are not baptized in the Spirit, according to Finney, is that they do not *really* want the Spirit:

> The fact is that you do not, *on the whole*, desire the Spirit. This is true in every case in which you do not have the Spirit. . . . And so, *on the whole*, you do not wish to have the Spirit come, unless He will consent to dwell with you and let you live as you please. But that He will never do.[3]

Finney wrote elsewhere that "there is no difficulty in our obtaining the Holy Spirit if we are willing to have it, but this implies a willingness to surrender ourselves to his direction and discretion."[4] To desire and ask for the Baptism in the Spirit is to desire and ask for sanctification. Thus, if one is sincerely asking to be baptized in the Spirit, he must be sincerely willing to surrender to his sanctifying control. To desire and ask for the Spirit is also to desire and ask for empowering for ministry. Thus, a sincere request for the Baptism in the Spirit must imply a true consecration to the task of evangelizing the world and acceptance of Christ's commission.[5] God, then, gives the Holy Spirit, not merely to those who ask but those who ask sincerely, truly desiring the object of their request.[6]

Finney believed further that prayer for the Holy Spirit must not only be sincere, it must be unselfish. One must pray with pure motives. "We must sympathize with God's reasons for our having the Spirit."[7] This point found illustration in Finney's memoirs, in the following conversation recorded there:

> (Mr. B–) said to me, "Mr. Finney what should you think of a man that was praying week after week for the Holy Spirit and could get no answer?" I replied that I should think he was praying from false motives. "But from what motives," said he, "should a man pray? If he wants to be happy, is that a false motive?" I replied, "Satan might pray with as good a motive as that," and then quoted the words of a Psalmist: "Uphold me with thy free spirit. Then will I teach transgressors thy ways and sinners shall be converted unto thee." "See!" said I, "the Psalmist did not pray for the Holy Spirit that he might be happy, but that he might be useful, and that sinners might be converted to Christ."[8]

Believers must not only ask sincerely and unselfishly, but with their asking they must yield to the Holy Spirit's influence. Many people pray for the Holy Spirit, but, in all their praying, they do not yield to his leadings.[9] Those who thus resist and grieve the Holy Spirit cannot receive him.[10] Finney said that

> if you would be baptized with the Holy Spirit you must fasten upon the promises of Christ and take hold of them in faith, laying your whole soul open to receive his influences . . . throw the mind open to His influences.[11]

In his *Lectures on Revivals*, Finney wrote,

> If you mean to have the Spirit, you must be childlike and yield to His influences—just as yielding as air. If He is drawing you to prayer, you must quit everything to yield to His gentle strivings. . . . If you wish (the Spirit) to remain you must yield to His softest leadings, watch to learn what he would have you do and yield yourself up to His guidance.[12]

This yielding is related to the sincerity of one's request. To pray for the Holy Spirit to fill and anoint one's life while resisting his influence and control is hypocritical.

Finney also emphasized the necessity of persistence or endurance in praying for the Holy Spirit.[13] Persistence in prayer is a sign of confidence in God's faithfulness and belief in His promises. Thus, Finney exhorts seekers:

> Rest with the utmost confidence in his promise to give you of the
> "fountains of water of life freely" and when you have taken hold of his
> promise, be sure not to let go or suffer your confidence to be shaken
> until you feel a consciousness that you are "baptized into his death."[14]

Many fail to receive the promise because of a lack of perseverance.

These conditions do not apply only to prayer for the Baptism in
the Spirit but to all prayer.[15] Finney related how, before his conversion,
he visited prayer meetings and the lack of answers to prayer or even
expectation of answers exhibited there nearly caused him to doubt
the truthfulness of Christ's teachings. He came to see, however, that
what he saw exhibited in these meetings was a failure to meet the
conditions of answered prayer revealed by God in Scripture.[16]

Meeting these conditions does not somehow earn God's favor or
the answers to our prayers. The reason for answered prayer is always
God's love and goodness. Our obedience to the conditions merely
removes the obstacles in the way, so that he may "let His infinite
benevolence flow out upon us without restraint."[17] God greatly delights
in pouring out his blessings and rejoices when we remove the
obstacles. The purpose of prayer is not to convince God to pour out
his Spirit and other blessings, but rather to put Christians in a state
in which God may freely bless them in a manner consistent with his
character and government.[18]

Prayer, then, is not the mere mouthing of certain requests, but a
turning to God with our whole being. Its purpose is not to change
God, but to change the one who prays. Prayer for the Holy Spirit
places the believer in a position of humility, expectancy, and
yieldedness, which is the necessary context in which the Spirit may
be given and experienced in fullness.

For Finney, these conditions are not works. He claims that the
Baptism in the Holy Spirit is received by "simple faith" in the promises
of God.[19] He stresses with great emphasis that sanctification is not
obtained by works or resolutions.[20] Nor is grace or faith obtained by
works.[21] Such works as fasting, prayer, Scripture reading, and outward
reformation of life will not produce faith, obtain grace, or achieve
sanctification. One must begin with faith, which alone purifies the
heart and from which all true holiness and virtue flows.[22] Only faith
unites one to Christ as the source of spiritual life and power.[23]

How does Finney reconcile his emphasis that the Baptism in the
Spirit is received by faith, not works, with the several conditions he
mentions in connection with prayer for the Holy Spirit? There is no
conflict for Finney because such conditions are all aspects of faith

as he understands it. In his definitions of faith, he frequently emphasizes that it included the yielding of the will. He stressed that "faith itself is an active and not a passive state."[24] In the discussion on faith in his *Systematic Theology*, Finney says that faith is a phenomenon of will . . . the soul's act of yielding itself . . . the yielding and committal of the whole will and of the whole being to Christ.[25] In regard to faith in the promise of the Holy Spirit, Finney writes that

> faith itself is an act of the will—a trust, a confiding in, a yielding up of the whole being to the influence of truth. Faith, then, is the yielding up of our voluntary powers to the guidance, instruction, influences, and government of the Holy Spirit.[26]

Thus, for Finney, the various conditions he presents for the gift of the Holy Spirit are not in addition to faith but rather the various expressions of faith. Faith is particularly understood as yielding to God.

Finney's understanding of faith and conditions is echoed by J. Rodman Williams. Rather than speaking of "conditions," Williams refers to the "human context" in which the free gift of the Holy Spirit is sovereignly given by God.[27] He writes that the Holy Spirit is given in the context of obedience, prayer, expectancy, and yielding. In this discussion of context, however, he emphasizes that these are not to be understood as additions to faith.

> Thus as we now move on to observe the context in which the Spirit is given, we continue to stand within the sphere of faith. We do not add one iota to faith—as if it were faith plus something else. Rather are we now dealing with various expressions of faith within faith—constituents of faith, in a sense—so that the context is not extraneous to faith, but its vital demonstration.[28]

Williams, like Finney, especially emphasized yielding as an important expression of faith. He says,

> It would be difficult to overemphasize this whole matter of yielding. It is at the heart of receiving the gift of God's Holy Spirit. For it is only as a person lays himself totally at the disposal of God, holding back nothing, that the Spirit moves in to take full possession. . . . Yielding is an act of faith. It is not something beyond faith but is faith in its profoundest expression.[29]

This understanding of faith as yielding, found in Finney, is a helpful contribution to our understanding of faith. The Evangelical emphasis on faith as personal trust is an adequate definition of faith in his passive expression, particularly in regard to justification. Faith, however, is also active. As Gal. 5:6 says, "faith *worketh* by love." When we consider faith in relation to sanctification, Christian living, and ministry, we see that faith in these activities is more than a passive trust in Christ but is an active yielding to his divine inward influence. With such a broader definition of faith, we can more readily see how sanctification, as well as justification, is by faith not works. We can also realize that an emphasis upon yielding to the Spirit's control in order to be filled with his presence and power is not contradictory to our understanding of the Holy Spirit as a gift received by faith alone.

The criticism of "conditions" for the Spirit is not completely answered by showing those conditions to be the various expressions of the sole condition of faith. Critics like Bruner and Warfield argue that the initial faith in the gospel receives the Holy Spirit in all his fullness and there is no need for a subsequent faith.[30] This actually raises again the question of subsequence discussed in the previous chapter. Williams provides a response to this type of criticism by emphasizing that faith is a "dynamic moving reality" which grows and increases from the moment of initial faith, leading the believer into fuller experiences of God's grace. Somewhere along the way of faith, sometimes at the onset, somemtimes subsequently, is a moment in which the Holy Spirit is received. All along the way, however, the object of faith is Jesus Christ.[31]

Finney, too, saw faith as dynamic. Faith grows and increases as the knowledge of Christ increases:

> With some the mind is comparatively weak in its first exercise. . . . Hence their trust in Him will be as narrow as their realizing convictions. When faith is weak, the current of the divine life will flow so mildly that we are scarcely conscious of it. But when faith is strong and all embracing it lets a current of the divine life of love into our souls so strong that it seems to permeate both soul and body.[32]

Establishment in the life of continual obedience through Spirit Baptism seldom takes place at the moment of conversion, but usually later as faith and knowledge have developed.

> When first converted, if we knew enough of ourselves and of Christ thoroughly to develop and correct the action of the sensibility, and confirm our wills in a state of entire consecration, we should not fall. . . . In most, if not all instances, however, the convert is too ignorant of himself, and of course knows too little about Christ to be established in permanent obedience.[33]

It is only after conversion, as faith and knowledge grow, that one begins to hunger and thirst for spiritual and moral purity and the experience of living union with Christ. It is in that state that the believer seeks and receives the Baptism in the Spirit.[34] Given Finney's experiential understanding of Spirit Baptism, one can easily see that this experience would usually come subsequent to the moment of initial faith, as faith develops.

The problem that Bruner has with such a view is probably a reflection of the admitted influence of Luther upon his theology.[35] As a result of this influence, Bruner seeks to understand salvation entirely in terms of justification. Thus, he writes,

> God's justification of the sinner is the meaning of the New Testament. (And sanctification from the believer's side is simply taking justification seriously.) The deep realization of the forgiveness of sins is the essential meaning of the gift of the Holy Spirit.[36]

The "Pentecostal passion for more," specifically, "more of spiritual experience" reflects their "under-evaluation of the forgiveness of sins," according to Bruner. This, he says, is "the heart of the Pentecostal problem."[37] Herein is seen one important area in which men and movements influenced by Wesley and Finney differ from their Lutheran and Reformed critics such as Bruner and Warfield—that is the view of justification not as encompassing the whole of salvation, but as the foundation of regeneration, sanctification, and union with Christ. Thus, Finney claims that "the main business of Jesus is to save him from the commission rather than the pardon of his sins."[38] Justification then is simply the beginning of God's work and there is more to be experienced and received by faith subsequent to justification. Finney would not disparage or belittle the wonderful blessing of justification or the importance of the beginning of faith, but would simply encourage new believers to continue in faith and receive all of God's promised blessings, including the Baptism in the Holy Spirit.

In concluding this discussion it must be noted that for Finney, while faith is an active expression of human will, it is always and at every stage induced and produced by the Holy Spirit.[39] Finney emphasizes that

> we are shut upon to God for faith—to the sovereign working of God's Holy Spirit, and the sovereign grace of God as manifested through Christ to produce this faith. Not that it is not our own exercise; it is indeed, and from its nature must be, but we must be sensible that without the Spirit of Christ we shall no more exercise this faith, than we shall get into heaven by our own works of obedience to law.[40]

Thus, that faith by which one receives the Holy Spirit is itself produced by the Holy Spirit as a gift from God.

•7•

FINNEY AND OTHER VIEWS OF SPIRIT BAPTISM:
A HISTORICAL AND COMPARATIVE STUDY

T HIS CHAPTER, will examine the historical relationship between Finney's view of the Baptism in the Holy Spirit and later views. Further, through contrast and comparison with these views, it will provide a fuller understanding of Finney's view, as well as encourage an appreciation for contributions Finney may offer to present-day views of the Baptism in the Holy Spirit. In addition, I will point to some positive critiques of Finney's view suggested by some of these later movements.

The various views of the Baptism in the Spirit which developed in the late-nineteenth and early twentieth centuries may be divided into four: the Wesleyan-Holiness view, the Keswick view, the Evangelistic view (held by D. L. Moody and R. A. Torrey), and the Pentecostal-Charismatic view. All of these, and especially the first three, are often grouped together as various expressions of the transdenominational Evangelical-Holiness movement. However, these groups may be distinguished when we look carefully at their precise understanding of the Baptism in the Holy Spirit. The Keswick movement, though it may be seen as a non-Wesleyan branch of the Holiness movement, developed a distinct view of sanctification and the "second blessing" and must be considered separately from that movement within Methodism. In the beginning, there may have been more of an overlap and less distinction, but in the following discussion we will look at these movements as their distinctive views ultimately developed. Similarly, Torrey and Moody, whose view of the Baptism I call "Evangelistic" because of its stress on power for evangelism rather than sanctification, are often included in the Keswick movement. Keswick men spoke at Moody's Northfield Conferences and Torrey spoke in some Keswick conferences. However, the emphasis upon empowering rather than sanctification as the purpose of Spirit Baptism differentiates their view from the general emphasis of Keswick. The

Pentecostal view, with its emphasis on speaking in tongues, is clearly distinct from the above. So, in the following section I shall discuss each of these separately, beginning with the Wesleyan-Holiness view.

FINNEY AND THE WESLEYAN-HOLINESS VIEW OF THE BAPTISM IN THE HOLY SPIRIT

According to Timothy Smith, "the man chiefly responsible for the adoption among holiness people in America and England of the terms 'filling' or 'baptism of the Spirit' to describe the experience of entire sanctification was Charles G. Finney."[1]

This involved a transition from earlier thought within the Methodist-Holiness movement which Donald Dayton describes in the article, "From Christian Perfection to the Baptism of the Holy Ghost."[2] John Wesley himself did not refer to the experience of sanctification or Christian perfection as the Baptism in the Holy Spirit. Dayton, relying on a study by Herbert McGonigle, claims that Wesley's major emphasis was christological rather than pneumatological.[3] Leo George Cox, on the other hand, argued that since Wesley believed in complete sanctification as an instantaneous gift from God and that sanctification was the work of the Spirit, the idea of sanctification through Baptism in the Spirit is implicit in Wesley's theology.[4] Even he admits, however, that "Wesley hesitated to call this experience the 'receiving of the Holy Ghost.' " "Others may do so if they wish," Wesley said, "but the phrase is not scriptural and not quite proper for they all 'received the Holy Ghost' when they were justified."[5] Wesley's associate, John Fletcher, however, did relate sanctification to the Baptism in the Spirit,[6] but even his view was somewhat ambiguous and did not have a great influence on early Methodism.[7] The renewed emphasis within Methodism upon Wesley's holiness teaching, which began in America in the 1830s under the leadership of Phoebe Palmer, Timothy Merritt, and others, did not in its early days use the language of Pentecost or Spirit Baptism. According to Dayton, the shift to such an understanding of sanctification began in the late 1850s and was nearly universal in the Holiness movement by 1900.[8]

Dayton recognizes the influence of Oberlin in this transition but stresses the writings of Finney's associates at Oberlin, Henry Cowles, John Morgan, and especially, Asa Mahan, rather than Finney. He finds Asa Mahan as having the most influence upon the Holiness movement, especially with the publication of his book *The Baptism of the Holy Ghost* in 1870.[9]

While rightly recognizing the work of the other Oberlin theologians,

Dayton was apparently unaware of Finney's early statements on the Baptism in the Spirit appearing in the *Oberlin Evangelist* in 1839–1840. The earliest of Finney's writings on the Baptism in the Spirit of which Dayton was aware was as late as 1871. Timothy Smith, on the other hand, in his study of the 1839–1840 series of articles, gives Finney the major credit for the shift in the Methodist-Holiness view of sanctification. He says:

> The transfer of Finney's Pentecostal language into American Methodism was direct and immediate. George O. Peck, editor of the influential Methodist weekly, the *New York Christian Advocate*, paid close attention to Finney's lectures as they appeared in *The Oberlin Evangelist* in 1839 and 1840. In the fall of the latter year, he became the first Methodist I know since John Fletcher to have equated the experience of entire sanctification with the Baptism of the Holy Spirit.[10]

Smith claims that as early as 1855 references to entire sanctification through being "baptized" or "filled" with the Spirit were frequent in reports of camp meetings and revivals in Methodist periodicals. While recognizing that, most probably, Finney developed his views in conjunction with his colleagues at Oberlin, and that Asa Mahan's ultimate influence upon the Holiness movement may have been the greatest, it does seem that Smith is correct in pointing to Finney as the one who initiated the shift within Wesleyanism to the language of Pentecost or Spirit Baptism to describe the experience of entire sanctification.

In light of this historical relationship, it is somewhat surprising to find later writers within the Wesleyan-Holiness movement criticizing the "Oberlin theology" of sanctification. H. Orton Wiley and Paul Culbertson's *Introduction to Christian Theology*, for example, rejects the Oberlin position, which is said to be represented by Asa Mahan, Charles Finney, and J. H. Fairchild, because of its denial of "inbred sin" as a "state or condition" and its identification of sanctification with consecration.[11] However, a close comparison of the Holiness view of the Baptism in the Spirit to that of Finney will prove that there is much greater agreement than difference.

First, though, it must be pointed out that any reference to "the Oberlin view of sanctification" as in the work referred to above, can be somewhat misleading. As Timothy Smith pointed out in *Revivalism and Social Reform*, there was a diversity of views proceeding from Oberlin.[12] There was a common emphasis on high standards of holiness and general agreement upon the possibility of attaining entire sanctification, but disagreement over the idea of a "second blessing."

Some believed that entire sanctification was attained through regeneration, and that there was no need for a second experience. Given Finney's view of the heart transformation effected by regeneration, one can see how such a view developed.

J. H. Fairchild, in particular, the successor of Mahan and Finney as president of Oberlin College, rejected Finney's view on the need for such a second blessing, as well as the possibility of permanent sanctification.[13] Fairchild argued that no one act of faith could ensure permanent sanctification. One can know if he is entirely sanctified, that is entirely consecrated, for the moment, by the testimony of one's consciousness. However, there is no way, he said, that one could know that he would remain consecrated permanently. Furthermore, God only requires sanctification from moment to moment. He does not require future sanctification in the present. Fairchild stressed the moment-to-moment consecration of life and the process of growth in sanctification rather than crisis experiences.

In response to Fairchild's criticisms, a brief clarification of Finney's view is in order. He wrote:

> No one act of faith, nor any other exercise can render salvation from sin or hell unconditionally certain. This is manifest from the fact that warnings and threatenings are every where addressed to the saints; which would be absurd, if their justification or sanctification were already unconditionally certain.[14]

Finney claimed:

> Entire sanctification does not imply the impossibility of future sin. Entire and permanent sanctification does imply in fact that the sanctified soul will not sin. But the only reason why he will not is to be ascribed to the sovereign grace of God.[15]

Finney's view was not that the one act of faith, by which one received the Baptism in the Spirit, rendered future sin an actual impossibility, but rather that through this experience one entered into a union with Christ which provided the needed divine grace to overcome sin, as the believer continued to abide in Christ. The Baptism in the Spirit did not render future sin impossible but rather made unceasing obedience possible. While I am sympathetic to Fairchild's emphasis on the process of sanctification and his questioning the possibility of permanent sanctification, I believe he fails to see the importance of crisis experience in the process of sanctification and does not recognize that such experience will have a continuing effect in the believer's life. Whether valid or not, Fairchild's criticisms do illustrate that one cannot speak of a unified Oberlin view on sanctification.

An earlier biographer of Finney, a Holiness leader, teacher, and theologian, as well as a former Oberlin student, A. M. Hills recognized the differences between Finney and Fairchild but criticized Finney's own view of sanctification, nonetheless. He believed that Finney approximated but never fully grasped the Wesleyan understanding of the Baptism in the Holy Spirit.[16] Finney wrote that he rejected the Methodist view of sanctification even though he recommended Wesley's writings.[17] A closer look, however, reveals much more agreement than disagreement between Finney and the Holiness view.

Hills criticized Finney's view, because Finney "fixed all his attention upon the will as the only faculty of the man that needed any attention in seeking holiness."[18] Finney rejected the Methodist view because it seemed to him to relate sanctification to the states of the sensibility. According to Hills, this was reflective of the fundamental error in Finney's thought, a lack of concern over the sanctification of the sensibility. Finney lacked a view of sanctification which involved "slaying those propensities and appetites due to natural depravity which are hostile to God and holiness."[19]

While it is true that Finney defined sanctification strictly in terms of the consecration of the will, it is also true that he believed that the Baptism in the Holy Spirit is directed precisely toward "slaying those propensities and appetites" which hinder the consecration of the will.

> One great thing that needs to be done, to confirm and settle the will in an attitude of entire consecration to God, is to bring about a counter development of the sensibility so that it will not draw the will away from God. . . . This can easily be done through and by the Holy Spirit who takes of the things of Christ and shows them to us.[20]

Finney does differ from the Methodists in that the involuntary states of the sensibility or intellect, the feelings, desires, and appetites, cannot, strictly speaking, be considered sinful. These are expressions of physical or natural depravity and have no moral character. It is only moral depravity or depravity of the will or sinful moral choice that is sin.[21] The Holiness theologians, on the other hand, would refer to "natural depravity" as "indwelling sin."[22] However, even though Finney did not consider these involuntary states as sin, it is clear that he was aware of the powerful influence of these states over the will, and like the Wesleyans, Finney saw the Baptism in the Spirit as the means of transforming the believer's intellect and especially the sensibility or emotional faculty so that it might not be a source of stumbling.

This finds illustration in Finney's sermon on "Prayer for a Pure Heart" based on David's prayer in Psalm 51, "Create in me a clean heart." David's prayer, Finney said, presupposed that his will was consecrated to God. What David prayed for was

> a thorough cleansing or sanctification of the whole mind; including the regulation or cleansing of the imagination, the thoughts, desires, feelings, all those modifications if the sensibility and all those habitudes of thought and feeling which so often annoy the Christian and become most distressing and dangerous snares to his soul.[23]

According to Finney these "unsanctified involuntary states of mind" are "the fleshly lusts that war against the soul's peace and purity." These states ought not be described as "inborn or inbred sin." They are "not themselves sin but the occasions of sin—the means of temptation to sin." Finney explains:

> Sin strictly speaking, belongs to acts of the will only . . . when sin or moral defilement is predicated of other faculties or states of mind, the language is used in a popular and not a metaphysical sense."[24]

Christians may have their wills consecrated to God and yet, have considerable warfare with these involuntary states. They create within the believers' mind "a certain uneasiness and a sense of loathing as if they were really unclean." Further, if unchecked, they become the occasion of actual sin. Finney presents the cleansing of the sensibility as attainable and encourages his readers to pray in faith for this cleansing.

Again, it is clear that while Finney would disagree with the Holiness view of these involuntary states of the heart as sin, he does not disagree that this part of the individual needs cleansing and that God will provide the cleansing needed. Thus, A. M. Hills' criticism that Finney's view is defective in failing to deal with the "propensities and appetites" which influence the will is unfounded.

A second major criticism which Hills directed toward Finney was that he made sanctification synonymous with consecration.[25] While Finney usually defines sanctification in terms of entire consecration, his descriptions of this experience often point beyond to something more. It seems that from his understanding of God's moral government and the principles of moral law under that government, Finney could only describe sanctification in terms of consecration of the will; but, from the perspective of Christian experience, Finney finds sanctification to include something beyond consecration. As described above, Finney viewed sanctification as a cleansing and transforming of the sensibility. Furthermore, sanctification was a state of experiential union with Christ through the indwelling Holy Spirit. In the sermon on "Prayer for the Holy Spirit," Finney said that to be sanctified "is to be filled with the Holy Ghost, so that he takes full possession of our souls."[26] This, he said, implies something beyond entire consecration:

> When the will is really on God's altar, entirely yielded up to God's will in all respects, one will not wait long ere he has the Spirit of God in the fullest measure. Indeed this very consecration itself implies a large measure of the Spirit, yet not the largest measure. The mind may not be conscious of that deep union with God into which it may enter. The knowledge of God is a consciousness of God in the soul. You may certainly know that God's Spirit is within you, that his light illumines your mind. His presence becomes a conscious reality.[27]

Thus, for Finney, like the Wesleyan theologians, sanctification goes beyond consecration in the believer's experience. So, even though Finney disagreed with the Methodists over the question of whether involuntary states may be called sin, he agreed with them that the Baptism in the Holy Spirit provides a cleansing and transformation of those states. Furthermore, this cleansing and the conscious union with Christ which results from Spirit Baptism, for Finney, along with the Wesleyans, goes beyond consecration of the will.

FINNEY AND THE KESWICK VIEW OF THE SPIRIT AND SANCTIFICATION

A parallel movement to the emphasis on sanctification and perfection within Methodism arose among Evangelicals outside of Methodist circles. The earliest leaders of the movement, William Boardman, Robert Pearsall Smith, and Hannah Whitall Smith, were Americans, but the movement came to be centered in England. Out of this "Higher Life" movement, beginning in 1875, an annual conference met in England at a place called Keswick. Keswick conferences continue to this day, not only in England but throughout the world. Timothy Smith suggests that Finney played a role in the development of this "Keswick movement," in which many Anglicans, Presbyterians, Baptists, and others came to adopt views on sanctification very similar to those promoted by the Wesleyan and Oberlin theologians. In the histories of the Keswick movement, though, one does not find references to Finney, though his colleague at Oberlin, Asa Mahan, was very much involved in this movement.[28] However, it is not unreasonable to suggest, as Smith does, that Finney's English evangelistic tours of 1849 and 1858–1861, together with the publication of his writings in that country, paved the way for the Higher Life teaching of Boardman and the Smith's in the 1860s and 1870s.[29]

The distinct feature of the Keswick theology of sanctification, in comparison to Wesleyan-Holiness or Oberlin ideas, was the Keswick attempt to maintain a traditional Reformed understanding of sin. Thus, the Keswick teachers would agree with the Wesleyans that those involuntary states which Finney denied to be sin are indeed sin. The "tendency to sin" within humanity or that "indwelling principle of sin" is itself sin. Unlike the Wesleyans, the Keswick teachers affirm that this tendency to sin is never eradicated in this life. Sin as a tendency or principle will always be present in the life of the believer.[30]

Nonetheless, the Keswick movement emphasizes that through the Holy Spirit the believer may experience continual victory over sin. Unlike Finney, most of the Keswick teachers related the "Baptism of the Spirit" with regeneration. The life of victory comes through the Christian's appropriation of the "fullness of the Spirit."[31] Some, however, did refer to this "fullness" as "the Baptism in the Holy Spirit."[32] Whatever it may be called, the Keswick teachers, just like Finney, saw this as a definite experience usually subsequent to regeneration.[33]

The Keswick movement is very close to Finney with its understanding of sanctification as both christocentric and pneumatological, and with its emphasis on sanctification as a state of continual dependence on Christ. The basis for sanctification is the believer's union with Christ.[34] This union is made experiential by the agency of the Holy Spirit. As mentioned above, the work of the Spirit is not to "eradicate" the sinful tendencies within the believer. Nor is it to "suppress" them. "God's method of sanctification is not suppression or eradication but counteraction."[35] The power of sin is counteracted by the greater power of the indwelling Holy Spirit. A favorite text in the Keswick movement, illustrating this point, was Rom. 8:2, "The law of the Spirit of life in Christ Jesus hath made me free from the law of sin and death." This verse is explained as follows:

> Deliverance (from the law of sin and death in our bodies) is by a new law, a mightier force, which counteracts the power of the law of sin. As real as is the energy of sin working our members, and more mighty is the energy of the Holy Spirit dwelling in our bodies.[36]

Thus, the believer is ever dependent upon the indwelling Spirit of Christ to counteract the ever-present tendency to sin and to enable one to maintain a life of victory.

> Apart from Christ as our indwelling life even the most advanced believer would at once relapse into his former condition, because the tendency to evil would no longer be counteracted. This teaches us that in ourselves, we have nothing to glory in—that our holiness does not consist in a state of purity which we can possess apart from Christ. Nor that our blessedness arises from any supposed freedom from the natural tendency to sin, but rather from the glorious fact that Christ is stronger than Satan and sin, and that when He takes full possession of the soul, He so completely overcomes all the evil and meets the force of its power that the believer is no longer hindered in his progress or robbed of his peace.[37]

This is similar to Finney's view as illustrated in the following passege:

> Many persons . . . are so blinded as to suppose that a soul entirely sanctified does not any longer need Christ, assuming that such a soul has spiritual life in and of himself, that there is in him some foundation or efficient occasion of continued holiness, as if the Holy Spirit had changed his nature, or infused physical holiness or an independent holy principle into him, in such a sense that he has an independent well-spring of holiness within, as a part of himself . . . . When will such men—when will the Church understand that Christ is our sanctification; that we have no life, no holiness, no sanctification, except as we abide in Christ, and He in us; that Christ does not change the constitution of man in sanctification, but that he only, by our own consent gains and keeps the heart; that He enthrones Himself, with our consent, in the heart and through the heart extends His influence and His life to all our spiritual being.[38]

One great difference between the theology of Finney and Keswick theology is, that whereas Finney only emphasized the believer's present union with the resurrected Christ, the Keswick teachers emphasized also the believer's union with Christ's historic death and resurrection.

> Calvary, Keswick tells us, is God's answer to the whole problem of sin. Christ's purpose in going to the cross was to deal drastically and decisively with sin in all of its aspects. In the whole matter of man's salvation everything begins at the cross. This is true of sanctification as well as justification. Man cannot become holy without the cross. The ground of the believer's sanctification is his identification with Christ in his death to sin.[39]

The Kewsick movement placed great emphasis upon the sixth chapter of Romans, calling it "the Magna Carta of the Christian" which declares the believer's freedom from sin through his union with Christ in his death and resurrection. This deliverance, having taken place at the cross, is "an already established fact."[40] Therefore, the work of the Holy Spirit in sanctification is dependent upon the cross:

> If the cross is the ground, the Holy Spirit is the agent of our sanctification. It is the office and work of the Holy Spirit to make true in our experience that for which Christ died for us on the cross . . . [the Holy Spirit] renders real and operative our death to sin and life to God. . . . In the process of sanctification, the Holy Spirit never works apart form the cross. He brings us into the path of freedom by beginning at the cross. He does not obtain our freedom from sin's dominion in the sense in which Christ has secured it for us, but by bringing us into it as something already obtained. . . . What Christ purchased for us, the Spirit imparts to us.[41]

Finney failed to recognize our union with Christ in his crucifixion as the foundation and basis of the Spirit's work in sanctification. He interpreted the references to this union in Romans 6 much more metaphorically, as is illustrated in the following comments on Rom. 6:11:

> The analogy between Christ's death in relation to sin and our dying to sin goes to this extent and no farther: He died for the sake of making an atonement for sin and for the sake of creating a moral power that should be effective to kill the love of sin in our hearts, but the Christian dies to sin in the sense of being divorced from all sympathy with sin and being emancipated from its control.[42]

In Finney's theology, the role of the cross in sanctification is to exert a powerful moral influence through its demonstration of God's love. The Keswick view is superior with its stress on the believer's real union with Christ in his death and resurrection, for it thereby roots the experience of union with Christ and the work of the Holy Spirit in salvation history. Justifying and sanctifying grace and objective and subjective soteriology are thus joined together at the cross of Christ.

The Keswick view seems to come closer to the eschatological viewpoint of the New Testament. In the early Christian understanding, the inauguration of the new age of salvation and God's kingdom through Christ's saving work in history has accomplished the sanctification of God's people as an objective reality. This sanctification is then experienced subjectively through the ministry of the Holy Spirit and the faith of the Christian.[43] With its emphasis on the believer's accomplished sanctification, based on union with Christ in his death and resurrection, which is mediated by the Holy Spirit and received by faith, the Keswick movement seems to have recovered this New Testament viewpoint.

I believe the Keswick movement is also correct in its rejection of the perfectionism found in Finney and the Wesleyans. In the Keswick theology, the tendency to sin is itself sin. Sins of ignorance are truly sins as well.[44] Even the believer walking in victory

> is to pray with profound sincerity, "forgive us our trespasses," and to reflect on his need of cleansing from all sin by the propitiatory blood of Jesus Christ.[45]

The Keswick teachers allow a certain tension to remain, even as they stress God's abundant provision for victory.

> From the side of God's grace and gift, all is perfect, but from the human side, because of the effects of the Fall, there will be imperfect receptivity, and therefore imperfect holiness to the end of life.[46]

Again, Keswick seems close to the eschatological viewpoint of the New Testament for it reflects the tension found there between the new age of God's rule and salvation which has begun but is not yet consummated, and this present age which is passing away, yet continues. Thus there is a tension in the Christian life between the "indicative, . . . the affirmation of what God has done to inaugurate the new age" and "the imperative, . . . the exhortation to live out this new life in the setting of the old world."[47] Since the kingdom of God has truly come in Christ Jesus, "the righteousness of the reign of God can be actually and substantially experienced even in the present age." However, "the perfect righteousness of the Kingdom, like the Kingdom itself, awaits the eschatological consummation."[48] Keswick's emphasis upon a real participation in Christ's victory over the power of sin and an actual experience of that victory through the indwelling Holy Spirit expresses the New Testament affirmation of the reality of the presence of the kingdom. The Keswick awareness of the tension in the Christian's experience of Christ's victory over sin and the incompleteness of our present experience of righteousness, on the other hand, expresses the New Testament recognition that the present age of Satan, sin, and death persists; final consummation of the new age, and the believer's full and perfect experience of God's salvation, are still future.

In Keswick theology, the insights of Luther and Calvin into the extent of human sin are not lost, even while an emphatic emphasis upon God's abundant provision for the believer's victory over sin, characteristic of Finney and Wesley, is maintained. As a result, the

Keswick view of sanctification through the fullness of the Spirit is, I believe, much closer to the biblical viewpoint than Finney's view.

FINNEY, D. L. MOODY, AND R.A. TORREY: THE BAPTISM IN THE SPIRIT AS EMPOWERING FOR MINISTRY

Both the Wesleyan-Holiness movement and the Keswick movement emphasized the Baptism or fullness of the Holy Spirit in connection with sanctification. An emphasis on power for service is sometimes present, but secondary. There were other Evangelicals, however, for whom the Baptism in the Spirit was primarily, and almost exclusively, an empowering for ministry. Two important proponents of such a view were Finney's successors as nationally prominent American evangelists: Dwight L. Moody (1837–1899) and Reuben Archer Torrey (1856–1928).

While there is apparently no evidence of an influence by Finney or his writings upon Moody,[49] there is a close similarity between Moody's understanding of the filling of the Holy Spirit and Finney's teaching on the Baptism in the Holy Spirit as a divine empowering for evangelism. Moody himself experienced this baptism of power in 1871. Two Free Methodist women who attended his YMCA prayer meetings in Chicago had been praying for him and urging upon him his need for the "anointing of the Holy Ghost." He eventually began earnestly praying to be filled with the Holy Spirit. Later, in New York City, Moody had an indescribable spiritual experience which brought new power to his ministry and resulted in an even greater effectiveness in evangelism.[50] His subsequent teaching reflected this experience. He taught that even though all true believers are indwelt by the Holy Spirit from conversion, many, if not most, have failed to seek the anointing power for service which comes subsequent to conversion. "The Holy Ghost coming upon them with power is distinct and separate from conversion," claimed Moody.[51] Moody used such phrases as filling, anointing, and baptism to describe this work of the Spirit.[52]

Moody did not relate this experience to sanctification. He was opposed to perfectionism. Moody had some connections with Keswick. The beginning of the Keswick movement was coincident with his English evangelistic tours, and Keswick men spoke at Moody's Northfield Conferences. However, a biographer claims that Moody was very cautious toward the movement because of its possible perfectionist tendencies. For Moody, the Baptism in the Holy Spirit was exclusively related to ministry, not sanctification.[53]

R. A. Torrey claimed that one of the secrets of why God used D. L. Moody in such a mighty way was that "he had a very definite enduement with power from on high, a very clear and definite baptism with the Holy Ghost."[54] According to Torrey, Moody frequently asked him to preach on the "baptism with the Holy Ghost."[55] Torrey, too, had experienced a Baptism of the Spirit bringing a new anointing of power upon his ministry.[56]

Torrey presented his view of the Baptism in the Holy Spirit in several books.[57] In these books, he emphasized that this Baptism is a definite experience.[58] It is separate and distinct from regeneration, though regeneration and Spirit Baptism may sometimes occur simultaneously. The purpose of the Baptism with the Holy Spirit "is always connected with testimony and service . . . not . . . for the purpose of cleansing from sin, but for the purpose of empowering for service."[59] Torrey says that there is a work of the Holy Spirit to cleanse from sin by giving victory over the carnal nature, but that is not the purpose of the Baptism with the Spirit.[60] In his book, The Person and Work of the Holy Spirit, Torrey has a chapter on "The Holy Spirit Setting the Believer Free from the Power of Indwelling Sin," which is along similar lines as the Keswick teaching.[61] In his chapter on the Baptism in the Spirit in the same work, however, Torrey stresses that the purpose of the Baptism is "not primarily to make believers individually holy . . . but the primary purpose of the Baptism with the Holy Spirit is efficiency in testimony and service."[62] This emphasis is similar to Finney's view in those writings in which he presented the Baptism in the Spirit as an enduement of power from on high. A biographer mentions that Torrey was greatly influenced by Finney's writings, particularly his autobiography and Lectures on Revival.[63] It was in his autobiography that Finney referred to the Baptism in the Spirit as "the indispensable qualification of a successful ministry" and "that divine anointing" which gives a minister "power in the pulpit and in society for the conversion of souls."[64] Several references to the example of Finney's Baptism in the Spirit are found in Torrey's books on the subject.[65]

Torrey, like Finney, also stressed the need for "fresh baptisms with the Holy Spirit." Torrey wrote:

> For each new service that is to be conducted, for each new soul that is to be dealt with, for each new service for Christ that is to be performed, for each new day and each new emergency of Christian life and service, we should definitely seek a new filling with the Holy Spirit.[66]

Torrey, unlike Finney, argued that the term "baptism" should be reserved only for the initial experience, and all succeeding experiences should be termed "fillings with the Holy Spirit."

Torrey was apparently influenced by Finney's emphasis on the Baptism in the Spirit as an empowering for ministry, and it is through Torrey that this particular emphasis of Finney gained wide acceptance among Evangelicals and particularly Pentecostals. Since the dominant emphasis in the Pentecostal view of the Baptism in the Spirit is "power" rather than sanctification, it is probable that the main line of influence from Finney to Pentecostalism runs through Torrey rather than the Holiness movement.

The emphasis on empowering and ministry in Finney, Moody, and Torrey is positive in that it moves the focus of the Spirit's work in the believer beyond his individual experience to his mission in the world. Particularly in Finney, this mission goes beyond the saving of souls to the transformation of society. The Baptism in the Holy Spirit thus becomes a radical experience which brings the transforming power of God, not only to the individual, but through his anointed ministry, into the world. This emphasis on empowering is clearly scriptural. Scripture presents the risen Christ, referring to the Pentecostal experience, as saying, "You shall receive power after that the Holy Spirit has come upon you and you shall be my witnesses" (Acts 1:8).

The weakness in this emphasis on empowering is that the sanctifying dimension of the Baptism in the Holy Spirit may be lost sight of, as it is in Moody and Torrey. A further danger, present in all three of these Evangelists, is that success in ministry becomes the sign of the presence of the Holy Spirit. Clearly, an apparently successful ministry and large numbers of converts may be present where the Holy Spirit is not. Conversely, the presence and power of the Holy Spirit may be manifested in some situations, not by success, but by faithfulness and endurance in the midst of failure and suffering.

FINNEY AND THE PENTECOSTAL VIEW OF THE BAPTISM IN THE HOLY SPIRIT

F. D. Bruner claims that the man

who has placed after Wesley, the most indelible stamp upon Pentecostalism was a man born a year after Wesley's death—Charles Finney.[67]

Bruner's view, however, is that it was Finney's revival methods more than his doctrines that have influenced Pentecostalism. He says,

> Finney's influence on subsequent Pentecostalism may be said to have been, in fact, more in the realm of form and "temperature" than in the realm of content and ideas.[68]

Whether that be true or not, the question of relationship in the "realm of ideas" remains, and so we shall compare Finney's doctrine of the Baptism with the doctrine of Pentecostalism.

At the great Azusa Street Revival in California from which Pentecostalism exploded throughout the world in the early 1900s, Christians from various backgrounds came into the experience of the Baptism in the Holy Spirit with the evidence of speaking in tongues. Whether their background was in the Holiness movement or the Keswick movement, or if they had been influenced by Torrey's writings, all of these early Pentecostals could trace their spiritual ancestry to Charles Finney. As we have seen, Finney was the first important figure to emphasize the Baptism in the Holy Spirit as a subsequent experience, and in at least some way, he influenced all of these various movements within late-nineteenth century Evangelicalism thereby providing the source of Pentecostalism. Thus, we may call Finney the grandfather of Pentecostalism.

The convergence and transformation of these various Evangelical movements in Pentecostalism may be illustrated by a brief overview of the rise of the movement.[69] The earliest Pentecostals came from the Wesleyan-Holiness movement. This was true of such early leaders as Charles Parham, William Seymour, C. H. Mason, Frank Bartleman, G. B. Cashwell, J. H. King, and A. J. Tomlinson. By 1900 the Holiness movement had broken from the Methodist church, creating many new denominations. Several of these were to later become Pentecostal denominations.[70] The stage was set for the rise of Pentecostalism within the Wesleyan-Holiness movement by Benjamin Hardin Irwin, founder of the Fire-Baptized Holiness Church. Irwin advocated the view that the Baptism in the Holy Spirit was a third experience, following conversion and sanctification. This "Baptism with the Holy Ghost and Fire" brought power to those who had been cleansed and prepared for it by the experience of sanctification.

Charles Parham held to such a view when he instructed the students in his Holiness Bible School in Topeka, Kansas, to search the Scriptures for the biblical evidence for this third experience. The students concluded from studying the Book of Acts that speaking in tongues was the evidence of the Baptism in the Spirit, and thus the doctrinal basis for the Pentecostal movement was established. Soon after this discovery, Parham and all his students experienced tongue-speaking. Parham's school later moved to Houston, Texas, where a black Holiness preacher, W. J. Seymour, heard and adopted Parham's new teaching. It was Seymour who carried the message to Los Angeles. In his meetings on Azusa Street, a revival began that lasted three and one-half years. Innumerable people came to Azusa Street and received the Baptism in the Spirit with the evidence of speaking in tongues and then carried the new teaching home with them. Thus, Pentecostalism rapidly spread throughout the nation and the world.

Many of those who came to Azusa Street and received the Pentecostal Baptism were not Wesleyan in their background or theology. They viewed the Baptism, not as a third experience, following conversion and sanctification, but as a second experience understood more in terms of the teaching of Keswick or Torrey. The leader of the movement within Pentecostalism to discard the Wesleyan view of sanctification as a second work of grace prior to the Baptism in the Spirit was William H. Durham, Baptist pastor of the North Avenue Mission in Chicago. Durham received the Pentecostal Baptism in the Holy Spirit and spoke in tongues at Azusa Street in 1907 and carried the Pentecostal message back to Chicago and the Midwest. Durham's view of sanctification stressed "the finished work of Christ at Calvary" which the believer received at conversion. Thus, there was no need for a second work of sanctification prior to receiving empowering through the Baptism in the Spirit. Durham began preaching his view in a Pentecostal convention in Chicago in 1910. He also published his views in his monthly periodical, *The Pentecostal Testimony*. In 1911 he was a guest preacher at the Azusa Street Mission but he was thrown out by Seymour for preaching "the finished work heresy."

There were, by this time, large numbers of independent Pentecostal preachers and congregations who, like Durham, could not accept the Wesleyan view of sanctification, and who refused to join the new Wesleyan-Pentecostal denominations. Many of these met in Hot Springs, Arkansas, in 1914 and formed a new denomination, the Assemblies of God, which has become the nation's largest Pentecostal denomination.

We shall look at the Assemblies of God *Statement of Fundamental Truths* for a representative expression of the Pentecostal view of the Baptism in the Holy Spirit and compare that view to Finney's. It states that:

All believers are entitled to and should ardently expect and earnestly seek the promise of the Father, the baptism in the Holy Ghost and fire, according to the command of our Lord Jesus Christ. This was the normal experience of all in the early Christian Church. With it comes the enduement of power for life and service, the bestowment of the gifts and their uses in the work of the ministry (Luke 24:49; Acts 1:4, 8; I Cor. 12:1–31). This experience is distinct from and subsequent to the experience of the new birth (Acts 8:12-17, 10:44-46, 11:14-16, 15:7-9). With the baptism in the Holy Ghost come such experiences as an overflowing fullness of the Spirit (Jn. 7:37-39, Acts 4:8), a deepened reverence for God (Acts 2:43; Heb. 12:28), an intensified consecration to God and dedication to his work (Acts 2:42) and a more active love for Christ, for His Word, and for the lost (Mark 16:20).

The Baptism of believers in the Holy Ghost is witnessed, by the initial physical sign of speaking with other tongues as the Spirit of God gives them utterance (Acts 2:4).[71]

In this statement one finds the Pentecostal emphasis on "power." However, this power is related not only to "service" but to the Christian "life." This Baptism results in greater reverence, consecration, and love, according to this statement. Thus, similar to Finney, the Baptism in the Spirit is related in at least some sense to sanctification, as well as to empowering for service.

Finney's underlying christocentric emphasis was present as well in early Pentecostal theology. While not found in present Pentecostal doctrinal statements, such as the one quoted, as Peter Hocken has shown, this emphasis was frequent in early Pentecostal testimonies and teaching.[72] This can be illustrated by a Pentecostal pioneer of England, Smith Wigglesworth, who describes his own Baptism in the Spirit, which like Finney's experience, included a vision of Jesus Christ:

The fire fell. It was a wonderful time as I was there with God alone. He bathed me in power. I was conscious of the cleansing of the precious blood, and I cried out, "Clean! Clean! Clean!" I was filled with the joy of the consciousness of the cleansing. I was given a vision in which I saw the Lord Jesus Christ. I beheld the cross, and I saw Him exalted at the right hand of God the Father. I could speak no longer in English but I began to praise Him in other tongues as the Spirit of God gave me utterance.[73]

Hocken provides several quotes from early Pentecostal periodicals referring to the christocentric character of Spirit Baptism. For example, Stanley Frodsham wrote that, "The Pentecostal Baptism of the Holy Spirit brings a deeper and clearer revelation of our Lord and Savior Jesus Christ."[74] Other references taken from the Azusa Street periodical, The Apostolic Faith, claimed that,

> The baptism is the third person of the Trinity upon your soul that reveals Christ and takes the things of the Father and shows them unto you.[75]

> When He (the Holy Ghost) comes into a believer, He comes to tell them all about Jesus' salvation. He reveals Christ. He paints Him as the wonderful Son of God, the brightest gem the Father had in heaven—our only hope of salvation and reconciliation with the Father.[76]

Hocken concludes from this study of early Pentecostalism that the movement needs a fuller definition of the Baptism in the Holy Spirit than that found in the various Pentecostal confessions now in use, one which preserves the christocentric emphasis. He offers the following definition:

> The Baptism in the Holy Spirit is an outpouring of the Holy Spirit of God which results in: a) an inner knowledge of Jesus through revelation to the human spirit which enables the recipient to act in the power of the Spirit, b) first, Godward in praise, c) secondly, manward in bold proclamation including evangelism and in the exercise of the spiritual gifts.[77]

This definition Hocken argues, "has the advantage of describing both the inner spiritual content and the primary effects of the baptism."[78]

This emphasis within Pentecostalism on the Baptism in the Spirit as a revelation of Christ, rediscovered by Hocken, is very much in accord with Finney's view. "The Holy Spirit," Finney wrote,

> takes of the things of Christ and shows them to us. He so reveals Christ, that the soul receives him to the throne of the heart and to reign throughout the whole being.[79]

The consequence of this revelation is new purity and power.

While there are these similarities between the Pentecostal view and that of Finney, the great difference is immediately obvious, that is, the Pentecostal belief that the evidence of the Baptism in the Spirit is speaking in tongues. Finney did not speak in tongues. Some Pentecostals would like to find a reference to tongue-speaking in Finney's statement that he "bellowed out the unutterable gushings of [his] heart" when he was baptized in the Holy Spirit.[80] However, no evidence in any of Finney's other writings can be found to support that interpretation. He explicitly stated that the Baptism of the Spirit which the apostles received on the Day of Pentecost "did not by any means respect principally the working of miracles as some seem to have supposed."[81] Finney, no doubt, agreed with the statements of his Oberlin colleague Henry Crowles that the "miraculous gifts" were "temporary appendages of the Spirit's baptism," and that the fruits of the Spirit available to Christians of every age are "something incomparably greater and infinitely better than the gift of tongues."[82] Finney stated that "the power of miracles may or may not be incidental to the spiritual baptism, but it by no means constitutes any part of it."[83]

Finney claimed that the Holy Spirit helps the believer to pray, but it is not as if the Holy Spirit "immediately suggests to us words or guides our language."[84] This is directly contrary to the Pentecostal understanding of "praying in the Spirit" through speaking in tongues. However, despite the difference, there is some similarity between the views of Finney and the Pentecostals on "prayer in the Spirit." Finney's very literal understanding of Rom. 8:26 has already been referred to. The passage states that the Holy Spirit "maketh intercession with groanings that cannot be uttered" and Finney interprets this as teaching that

> the Spirit excites desires too great to be uttered except by groans—making the soul too full to utter its feelings by words, so that the person can only groan them out to God who understands the language of the heart.[85]

While there are differences, we find both in Finney and Pentecostalism the concept of effective Spirit-inspired, deeply felt prayer which transcends the limitations of human language and is understood by God alone.

On the experiential level, too, there are similarities between Finney's "groaning" in the Spirit and the Pentecostal praying in tongues. Finney's own initial experience of this type of prayer came in the midst of intercession when he was so full of feeling that he found human language inadequate and could only "groan with groanings loud and deep."[86] The initial experience of speaking in tongues is often very similar. The context is usually one of worship, and the individual finds himself or herself so full of praise and adoration that human language seems inadequate: full expression to those feelings are given only through praying in Spirit-inspired languages. For some, this "prayer language" has first come in the context of intercession very similar to Finney's experience.

While Finney's experience and theology only approached the Pentecostal experience and understanding of speaking in tongues, his theology of the Baptism in the Holy Spirit offers some valuable contributions to a Pentecostal understanding of the relationship of speaking in tongues to Spirit Baptism. The Pentecostal belief in tongues as the initial physical evidence of the Baptism in the Spirit has been defended largely on exegetical grounds, pointing to the accounts in the Book of Acts as precedents. What has been lacking is a theological argument which shows that tongues-speaking has a vital relationship to the purpose and nature of the Baptism in the Spirit. Finney's theology offers two approaches Pentecostals could use to present just such an argument.

The first begins with Finney's understanding of the Baptism in the Spirit as establishing the believer in an experiential union with Christ. One of the chief means of experiencing that union, according to Finney, is prayer. "The Holy Spirit in the hearts of saints" is said to be "pre-eminently a Spirit of prayer."[87] To be "filled with the Spirit" is to have "the Spirit of Prayer."[88] It is through Spirit-inspired prayer that

Christ comes and pours the overflowings of His own benevolent heart into His people and leads them to sympathize with Him as they never do in any other way."[89]

In Spirit-inspired prayer one experiences a union of will, of mind, and of feeling with the Lord. The Baptism in the Spirit is to be a doorway into such a new union with Christ, and to do so, it must be the doorway into a new dimension of prayer. Thus, from Finney's perspective, a case could be made for an integral relationship between praying in tongues and the Baptism in the Spirit. By imparting "the prayer language of the Spirit," the Holy Spirit brings a new and deeper union with Christ into the believer's experience. The Christian experiences prayer "from God to God" in a manner which transcends the intellect alone as one can express the deep feelings of God in a language given by God himself. One enters into an experiential union with the Father, Son, and Holy Spirit.

The second avenue of argument demonstrating the relationship between Spirit Baptism and speaking in tongues begins with Finney's understanding of the Baptism in the Spirit as an experience which introduces the believer to the realities of the spiritual realm. Through Baptism in the Spirit, the realm of the Spirit and spiritual truths become an experiential reality to the Christian. This emphasis is found in Finney's discussion of the Baptism in the Spirit as the means of sanctifying the sensibility and making it responsive to spiritual rather than carnal realities. Finney wrote:

The carnal mind is alive and awake to earthly and sensible objects, but dead to spiritual realities. The spiritual world needs to be revealed to the soul. The soul needs to see and clearly apprehend its own spiritual condition, relations, and wants. It needs to become acquainted with God and Christ, to have spiritual and eternal realities made plain, and present, and all absorbing realities to the soul. . . . This can only be done by the revelation to the inward man, by the Holy Spirit, of those great, and solemn, and overpowering realities of the "Spirit land" that lie concealed from the eye of the flesh.[90]

An awareness of the "realities of the Spirit land" to which Finney referred is presented as an important result of the experience of speaking in tongues in the careful study by Morton Kelsey. He states that "the whole realm of the supernatural, the spiritual becomes more real to the one who has had this experience."[91] He remarks that tongue-speaking is

one entrance into the spiritual realm; by giving access to the unconscious, it is one contact with non-physical reality which allows God to speak directly to man.[92]

Kelsey states that

glossolalia . . . is an experience of the most basic and central reality of life, the realm of the Spirit, of which so many people are unconscious and from which so many people are cut off.[93]

The greatest value of speaking in tongues according to Kelsey is that "it forces us to consider the posiblity of direct contact with non-physical or spiritual reality."[94]

Kelsey argues for the discarding of an Aristotelian-based naturalistic world view for a world view informed by the philosophical perspective of Plato and the psychological insights of Jung, as well as the evidence of post-Newtonian scientific thought, in which one acknowledges the possibility of real contact with an actual non-physical, spiritual realm. In fact, Kelsey would argue that it is essential for the survival of the human race that we become aware of this realm, which, even if denied on the conscious level, is always touching the unconscious.[95] One means by which the reality of this spiritual reality may break in upon someone, from the unconscious into the conscious, is through the experience of speaking in tongues. From this awareness, one can cooperate with this spiritual reality on the conscioius level and receive healing and wholeness.

Both Finney and Kelsey have seen the lack of real awareness of the spiritual realm to be a problem in the world, the church and among individual Christians. Whereas, Finney points to the Baptism in the Spirit as the means to an awareness of spiritual realities, Kelsey points not only to the filling of the Spirit[96] but to experiences of the supernatural such as speaking in tongues, healing, dreams, and visions. Moreover, in the New Testament we find such experiences connected with and accompanying the Baptism in the Spirit. On the Day of Pentecost, for example, we not only find speaking in tongues, but in Peter's sermon we also find prophecy, dreams, and visions mentioned as results of the outpouring of the Spirit. Later, in the second chapter of Acts, we find reference to the "signs and wonders" occurring in the midst of the Spirit-filled community.

If the Baptism in the Spirit is a revelation of spiritual reality, we can readily see that speaking in tongues and other miraculous manifestations should be an integral part of that experience. Since the central spiritual reality that the Holy Spirit reveals is Christ, the manifestation of a divinely given language of praise to him would be an appropriate such miraculous manifestation.

So, Finney's understanding of the Baptism in the Spirit can lead Pentecostals into a deeper understanding of this experience, as well as provide some theological basis of their belief in the importance of speaking in tongues as an integral aspect of the Spirit Baptism. Furthermore, as Hocken's study has shown, the early Pentecostals themselves recognized this Baptism as a revelation of Jesus, and thus a study of Finney's view can help Pentecostals recover aspects of their own tradition.

•8•

SUMMARY AND CONCLUSION

CHARLES G. FINNEY UNDERSTOOD the Baptism in the Holy Spirit as an experience of the Holy Spirit's presence and power subsequent to conversion. It brought a greater revelation of Christ that produces a deeper union with him. As a result of this experience, believers are established in their consecration and obedience, and are anointed with power in their prayer life and ministry.

As much as he believed in and stressed human ability and responsibility, Finney was acutely aware of the Christian's utter dependence upon the Holy Spirit for both sanctification and service. His optimistic views on the perfectability of individuals and society rested, not upon human ability, but upon the powerful grace of God freely offered to those who believe. Yet, Finney found the experience of Christians as a whole falling far short of those attainments promised by God to those living in the new covenant age. Most were unstable in their consecration and obedience, and are powerless and ineffective in prayer and ministry. Thus, Finney came to stress the need for this experience of the Spirit beyond regeneration and conversion. He found scriptural support for his belief in the subsequence of Spirit Baptism in the example of the apostles and in such passages as Eph. 1:13. The promises of the new covenant, Finney believed, also pointed to a work of the Spirit beyond regeneration. The Baptism in the Holy Spirit is received by faith, Finney said, but he emphasized that faith includes yielding to the Holy Spirit's guidance and control.

Finney's views on this subject crystallized in the years 1839–1840, during a time in which the attention of all the Oberlin theological instructors was focused upon the subject of sanctification. The view which Finney developed at this time, however, was a natural evolution of his earlier thought stemming from his own dramatic Baptism in the Spirit at the commencement of his Christian life. Finney believed in repeated Baptisms in the Spirit as a normal part of the Christian life, and he experienced several such Baptisms. One of these later experiences has been mistakenly pointed to as Finney's Baptism in the Spirit, but Finney himself claimed that he was baptized in the Spirit immediately following his conversion. He referred to this later experience as a "fresh" Baptism of the Spirit. From 1840 on Finney continued to preach, teach, and write on the Baptism in the Spirit, and some of the last writings before his death were on this subject.

Finney, the revivalist and theologian, can never be properly understood without appreciating and understanding this pneumatological emphasis within his theology. Some of his earlier critics criticized him for writing moral philosophy rather than Christian theology.[1] There is some truth to such criticisms. Finney understood God's relationship to humanity in terms of a moral government. Regeneration was described as a moral transformation. Righteousness was understood as willing the highest good of being and consecrating oneself to that end as the ultimate intent in life. In some ways this was a strength of Finney's theology and revivalism and it accounts for the social impact of his preaching. Christianity, however, is more than moralism. Contrary to his critics, though, I believe this study has shown Finney to be more than a moralist. He was both a moralist and a mystic. His emphasis on Christian experience, represented by his views on Spirit Baptism, take him beyond mere moralism and show him to have a fuller understanding of the nature of the Christian faith.

As a result of Finney's emphasis on the Baptism in the Spirit, he was a significant figure in the rise of the Holiness, Keswick, and Pentecostal movements. The Holiness and Keswick movements were particularly influenced by the connection of Spirit Baptism with sanctification, whereas other Evangelicals, most notably R. A. Torrey, were influenced by Finney's stress upon this Baptism as an anointing of power for ministry. The Pentecostal movement, with its emphasis on glossolalia and other spiritual gifts, seems to be a departure from Finney's view. However, in this movement we find a similar emphasis on power for both sanctification and service, and in the early Pentecostals, a christocentricity that is very close to Finney's view. Even the belief in speaking in tongues as the evidence of the Baptism in the Spirit is foreshadowed by Finney's understanding of praying in the Spirit via inarticulate groans and his connection of the "infilling of the Spirit" with the "Spirit of prayer." Furthermore, it is possible that Finney's understanding of the nature of the Baptism in the Spirit may provide a theological basis for the Pentecostal belief in glossolalia as an integral aspect of this experience.

Before mentioning the several positive contributions Finney offers to the contemporary movements that emphasize Spirit Baptism, I must point out the major weakness in his view, that is, Finney's view that the Baptism in the Spirit results in "permanent" sanctification or "perfection." In my discussion of the Keswick view and its similarities to the eschatological viewpoint of the New Testament, I pointed out that Finney's understanding of sanctification lacks that tension and incompleteness that must characterize the experience of those who, though they have a real participation in Christ's victory now, still live in a world in which sin is present and await the perfection which will come only at the consummation.

Theology must walk a careful balance at this juncture. One may so stress the continuing power and presence of sin as to negate the biblical emphasis on the Christian's present experience of Christ's victory over sin. On the other hand, one may so underscore the present experience of victory as to deny the Christian's typical continuing struggle with sin and longing for the final defeat of evil at Christ's return. Finney's post-millennialism is an illustration of the latter.

The weakness in Finney's perfectionism, without going into a complete analysis, lies in his definition of sin. Based upon his philosophical presuppositions, Finney limits sin to conscious willful violations of known law. Unlike Finney, even Wesley had a much more comprehensive understanding of sin. Though he, too, often defined sin as "willful transgression of a known law," Wesley also considered those "sins of ignorance, sins of infirmity, mistakes," and failures in outward performance which are present even in Christians who are entirely sanctified, to be at least in some sense truly sins and in need of Christ's atonement.[2] Finney claimed that sanctified Christians continued to be dependent upon the atonement, but only for their past sins,[3] whereas Wesley argued that even the sanctified Christian is in daily need of Christ's atonement to cover personal short-comings.[4]

The Finneyite criticism of this viewpoint would be that this more comprehensive definition of sin makes certain sins or types of sin beyond the individual's conscious control. Even Scripture, however, refers to unintentional sins which need to be atoned for (Lev. 4:27). In his discussion of the doctrine of sin, Paul Tillich refers to the tragic and moral dimensions of existence.[5] There is in Christianity, he says, an inescapable tension between these two dimensions. While Finney's theology stresses the moral dimension of sin, that is, sin as a matter of individual responsibility and accountability, he does not do justice to the tragic dimension of sin, that is, sin as an inevitable characteristic of humanity and its world after the Fall. Again, theology must be very careful to be balanced in affirming both the tragic and moral dimensions of sin, for an overemphasis on either negates the other.

Finney's faulty view of sin is a natural consequence of his philosophy of the unity of moral action, that there is one ultimate motive, entirely good or entirely evil at any one moment in a person's life. Such a view is clearly called into question by the investigations of psychology into the complexities of human consciousness and unconsciousness. On the other hand, Finney's understanding of righteousness in terms of ultimate choice or supreme intent does seem to express a biblical emphasis. Scripture does present righteousness in terms of a commitment to God and his kingdom as one's ultimate priority, and this is what Finney emphasizes. The problem with his view is that he equates that commitment with perfection. This commitment, which always falls short in actual performance, is pleasing and acceptable to God, not on the basis of natural law as Finney argues, but on the basis of God's mercy and the atonement provided by Christ.

I would agree with Finney that, through the Baptism in the Holy Spirit, one experiences a real participation in Christ's victory over sin, but I would say that this participation is neither entire nor permanent. On the other hand, though I deny that the believer's sanctification will be entire, I believe that through the Holy Spirit it will be substantial, and though I deny permanency, I affirm that the believer may experience consistency in obeying God. Notwithstanding those areas in which I disagree, I believe Finney can offer several positive contributions to a contemporary understanding of the Baptism in the Holy Spirit, which I shall now review.

First, Finney's understanding of Spirit Baptism as a definite experience is helpful in the debate over subsequence, at least in clarifying the question. The division on this issue seems to lie upon that question, "Is the Baptism in the Spirit an experience?" If the answer is yes, and I believe it is, this opens the possibility that this experience may be subsequent to the moment of initial faith or water baptism.

Finney's understanding of faith is also a helpful contribution to our understanding. His view of faith as "yielding" provides insight into the relationship of faith, not just to Baptism in the Spirit, but to Christian living and service as well.

The christocentric focus of Finney's understanding of Spirit Baptism is probably his most important contribution. The Baptism in the Holy Spirit is not something beyond Christ or more than Christ, but is more of Christ in our experience. In his view of sanctification, Finney joins together the pneumatological and christological emphases of Scripture by presenting the Holy Spirit as the Teacher who reveals Christ in such a way as to make real in the believer's experience his union with Christ.

Related to this is Finney's emphasis on the Holy Spirit and prayer. It is through the experience of prayer that one enters into this union. Thus, Spirit Baptism must involve a deepening of the prayer life resulting in deeper union with Christ. As I have suggested, this opens great possibilities to theological understanding within the Pentecostal-Charismatic movements.

While not accepting his perfectionism, I believe Finney's emphasis on Spirit Baptism as an experience which establishes the believer in obedience is helpful. Finney stresses the importance of the Baptism in the Spirit for sanctification, without diminishing the radical nature of regeneration, by presenting regeneration as that which changes the believer's heart and Spirit Baptism as the enabling power for persevering in that new life.

The way in which Finney understands the Spirit's work in sanctification is quite helpful. While his simple view of human psychology (intellect, will, sensibility) may seem inadequate today, his insight into human experience is still valid. The problem that the Christian encounters is often just as Finney described. A person's will is consecrated to God, but his or her emotions are greatly influenced by the things of the world and carnal considerations. As Finney said, the realities of the spiritual world and spiritual truths have little impact upon the believer. Thus, there is a struggle as people attempt to commit themselves to a spiritual life. They are greatly aided in this struggle, when as a result of an overwhelming experience of the Holy Spirit's presence and a Spirit-given revelation of Christ, they get such a taste of the reality of Christ and his saving power that even their emotions and desires are stirred and drawn after God. This results in greater power over sin and consistency in obeying God.

Finney's analysis fits the experience of many participants in the present Charismatic movement. While they believed in Christ and were committed to him before, after the Baptism in the Spirit, many have found Christ and the things of the Spirit to seem more real than ever, with the result that it is easier to believe and obey. Again, Finney's emphasis can help Pentecostals understand why supernatural manifestations are an integral part of Spirit Baptism.

Finney also emphasizes that the Baptism in the Spirit is an empowering for service, and thus its impact moves beyond the believer's subjective religious experience to his or her mission in the world, because the believer is encouraged with the promise of divine cooperation in his or her ministry. This is another positive and scriptural contribution, though, as I mentioned, we must be careful not to make an exact equation between the presence of the Spirit and success.

Finally, Finney's emphasis upon repeated Baptisms in the Spirit can be an important corrective today. This experience is not a final attainment. The Spirit-baptized Christian should not rest, satisfied in a present experience, but instead, the individual should hunger for fresh Baptisms, which bring a greater revelation of Christ and result in an increased holiness of life and power in prayer and service.

ENDNOTES

INTRODUCTION

¹Sidney E. Ahlstrom, A *Religious History of the American People* (New Haven: Yale University Press, 1972), p. 461.

²V. Raymond Edman, *Finney Lives On.* (Minneapolis: Bethany Fellowship, 1951), pp. 15, 65.

³Paulus Scharpff, *History of Evangelism*, trans. Helga Bender (Grand Rapids: Eerdmans, 1966), p. 108.

⁴James Michael Cafone, "The Role of the Holy Spirit in the Theology of Charles Finney" (Ph.D. dissertation, Catholic University of America, 1979), p. 11.

⁵Timothy L. Smith, ed., Introduction to *The Promise of the Spirit*, by Charles Finney (Minneapolis: Bethany Fellowship, 1980), pp. 1, 25.

⁶Frederick Dale Bruner, A *Theology of the Holy Spirit* (Grand Rapids: Eerdmans, 1970), pp. 40–42.

⁷Smith, "Introduction"; "The Doctrine of the Sanctifying Spirit: Charles G. Finney's Synthesis of Wesleyan and Covenant Theology," *The Wesleyan Theological Journal* 13 (Spring, 1978): 92–113; "Righteousness and Hope: Christian Holiness and the Millennial Vision in America, 1800–1900," *The American Quarterly* 31 (Spring, 1979): 21–45.

⁸Cafone, see note 4.

CHAPTER 1

¹Charles Finney, *Charles G. Finney: An Autobiography* (New York: Fleming H. Revell, 1980; (originally published as *Memoirs of Charles G. Finney*, 1876), p. 24.

²Ibid., p. 300.

³Ibid., p. 60.

⁴The primary source for Finney's life is his autobiography. The best biography is still G. F. Wright *Charles Grandison Finney* (New York: Houghton Mifflin and Co., 1891). Another helpful source, though not a complete biography, is William G. McLoughlin, *Modern Revivalism: Charles G. Finney to Billy Graham* (New York: The Ronald Press, 1959). Other biographies consulted were Richard Ellsworth Day, *Man of Like Passions: A Dramatic Biography of Charles G. Finney* (Grand Rapids: Zondervan, 1942); A. M. Hills, *Life of Charles G. Finney* (Cincinnati: M. W. Knapp, 1902).

⁵J. E. Johnson, "Charles Finney and a Theology of Revivalism" *Church History* 38 (1969): 357.

⁶Raymond Bailey, "Building Men for Citizenship" in *Preaching In American History*, ed. DeWitte Holland (Nashville: Abingdon, 1969), pp. 135, 138–40, 148.

⁷Ibid., p. 141.

[8]For discussions of Finney's social activism see Dayton, *Discovering An Evangelical Heritage* (New York: Harper and Row, 1976); Smith, *Revivalism and Social Reform in Mid-Nineteenth Century America* (Nashville: Abingdon Press, 1957).

[9]The Second Great Awakening is described in Ahlstrom, *Religious History of the American People*, pp. 415ff.

[10]Frank H. Foster, *A Genetic History of the New England Theology* (Chicago: University of Chicago Press, 1907).

[11]Joseph Haroutunian, *Piety vs. Moralism: The Passing of the New England Theology* (New York: Henry Holt and Co., 1932). The contrast between Foster and Haroutunian is pointed out by Ahlstrom, pp. 412–13.

[12]Charles Hodge "Review of Finney's Systematic Theology," *Biblical Repertory and Princeton Review* 19 (1847): 237ff, Warfield, *Perfectionism*, 2:166–215.

[13]This summary of the history of the New England Theology is based on the histories by Foster and Haroutunian; Ahlstrom, chaps. 19, 25, 26, 28; George M. Marsden, *The Evangelical Mind and the New School Presbyterian Experience* (New Haven: Yale University Press, 1970).

[14]Finney, *Autobiography*, p. 59.

[15]Equally applicable to Finney is the discussion on the Common Sense Philosophy and the theology of Nathanial Taylor in Marsden, *New School Presbyterian Experience*, pp. 47-49. For a discussion of Common Sense Philosophy and biblical interpretation see Marsden, "Everyone One's Own Interpreter: The Bible, Science and Authority in Mid-Nineteenth Century America" in *The Bible in America*, ed. Nathan Hatch and Mark Noll (New York: Oxford University Press, 1982), pp. 79ff.

[16]The basic source for Finney's theology is his *Lectures on Systematic Theology*, 2 vols. (Oberlin: James M. Fitch, 1846–47). An enlarged and revised one volume edition was later published in England—*Lectures on Systematic Theology*, ed. George Redford (London: William Tegg, 1851). The only major changes in the latter edition are the inclusion of replies to various criticisms of the first edition. References in this paper are to the English edition, though the sections discussed were compared to the original edition.

A condensed version of the English edition was later published as *Finney's Lectures on Systematic Theology*, ed. J. H. Fairchild (Oberlin: E. J. Goodrich, 1878). This was reprinted in 1951 by Eerdmans in Grand Rapids. An abridged verison of this edition, still in print, is *Finney's Systematic Theology* abridged (Minneapolis: Bethany Fellowship, 1976).

An introductory volume of theology first published in 1840 as *Skeletons of a Course of Theological Lectures* was reprinted by Bethany Fellowship in Minneapolis as *Finney's Lectures on Theology* in 1968 and *The Heart of Truth* in 1976.

For descriptions of Finney's theology see J. E. Johnson, "Charles Finney and a Theology of Revivalism"; McLoughlin, *Revivalism*, and Wright, *Charles G. Finney*. The historical context of Finney's theology is described by Smith in *Revivalism and Social Reform* and "Righteousness and Hope," *The American Quarterly* 31:21-45.

CHAPTER 2

[1]Warfield, p. 133.

[2]Dayton, "From Christian Perfection," p. 43.

[3]Smith, "Introduction."

[4]McLoughlin, p. 104; Smith, "Introduction," p. 24; "Doctrine of the Sanctifying Spirit," p. 105.

[5]Finney, Autobiography, pp. 12–18.

[6]Ibid., p. 23.

[7]Ibid., p. 20.

[8]Ibid.

[9]Ibid., pp. 20–21.

[10]Ibid., p. 21.

[11]For example, Dayton, "Christian Perfection to Baptism of the Holy Ghost," p. 43.

[12]Finney, Power From On High: A Selection of Articles on the Spirit–filled Life (Fort Washington, Pa: Christian Literature Crusade, n.d.), p. 9.

[13]Finney, Autobiography, p. 20.

[14]Ibid., p. 55.

[15]For example, Cafone, pp. 226–27.

[16]Hills, p. 21.

[17]Finney, Autobiography, pp. 373ff.

[18]Ibid., p. 373.

[19]Hills, p. 155.

[20]Finney, "Death to Sin," The Oberlin Evangelist 2 (July 15, 1840):#13. (The Oberlin Evangelist hereafter referred to as O.E.).

[21]Finney, Sermons on Gospel Themes (Manchester: James Robinson, n.d.), pp. 408–409.

[22]For example: Sermons on Important Subjects (New York: John S. Taylor, 1836).

[23]Finney, Promise of the Spirit, pp. 49–53, 259–60.

[24]Ibid., p. 262.

[25]Finney, Lectures on Revivals of Religion (New York: Fleming H. Revell, 1868).

[26]McLoughlin, p. 85.

[27]Finney, Revivals of Religion, p. 1.

[28]Ibid.

[29]Ibid., p. 110.

[30]Ibid., p. 1.

[31]Ibid., p. 10.

[32]Wright, p. 29.

[33]Ibid., pp. 29–30.

[34]Finney, Revivals of Religion, p. 137.

[35]McLoughlin, p. 107.

[36]Finney, Revivals of Religion, pp. 103, 105, 115–16.

[37]Ibid., pp. 111, 122, 131–33.

[38]Ibid., pp. 127–31.

[39]Ibid., pp. 94ff.

[40]Ibid., pp. 111–12, 117.

[41]Ibid., p. 104.

[42]Ibid., p. 70.

[43]Finney, Lectures to Professing Christians (New York: Fleming H. Revell, 1878), p. 358.

[44]Ibid., p. 352.

[45]Ibid., p. 363.

[46]Finney, *Autobiography*, pp. 350–351; Smith, "Introduction," p. 16.

[47]Finney, *Autobiography*, pp. 339–340; *Promise of the Spirit*, pp. 49–53.

[48]Finney, *Autobiography*, p. 341.

[49]Finney, *Promise of the Spirit*, p. 51.

[50]These articles appear in *The Promise of the Spirit*.

[51]Finney, *Promise of the Spirit*, p. 150.

[52]Ibid., p. 162.

[53]Ibid., p. 190.

[54]Ibid., pp. 162, 184.

[55]Ibid., p. 197.

[56]Ibid., p. 190.

[57]Ibid., p. 262.

[58]Ibid., p. 263; The same basic message was repeated in another letter the following year O. E. 2 (Sept. 29, 1841): 156–57.

[59]These articles appeared in the *Oberlin Evangelist* from January 1 to April 22, 1840.

[60]Finney, "Sanctification, No. 3" *O.E.* 2 (Jan. 29, 1840): 20; "Sanctification, No. 8" *O.E.* 2 (April 18, 1840): 57.

[61]Finney "Sanctification, No. 8" (April 18, 1840): 59.

[62]Finney, "Death to Sin" *O.E.* 2 (July 15, 1840): 113–14.

[63]Finney, *Autobiography*, p. 373.

[64]For example, Smith, "Introduction," p. 25.

[65]Finney, *Autobiography*, p.381.

[66]Ibid., p. 378.

[67]Ibid., p. 341.

[68]Finney, *Sermons on Gospel Themes*, pp. 398ff.

[69]Finney, *O.E.* (Jan. 29, 1845–Jun. 24, 1846), reprinted in *Reflections on Revival*, ed. Donald Dayton (Minneapolis: Bethany Fellowship, 1979).

[70]Dayton, Introduction to *Reflections*, p. 3.

[71]Finney, *Reflections*, pp. 70, 74.

[72]Smith, "Introduction," p. 32 (endnote 64).

[73]Finney, *Systematic Theology*, p. 699.

[74]Ibid.

[75]Ibid., pp. 735–36.

[76]Ibid., pp. 608, 756.

[77]Ibid., p. 637.

[78]Ibid., p. 635.

[79]Ibid., p. 736.

[80]Finney, *Sermons on Gospel Themes*, p. 409.

[81]Finney, *Sermons on the Way of Salvation* (Oberlin, Ohio: E. J. Goodrich, 1891), pp. 430ff.

[82]Finney, *Autobiography*, p. 141.

[83]Ibid., pp. 95–97.

[84]Ibid., p. 55.

[85]Ibid.

[86]Ibid., pp. 423–24.

[87]All of these tracts cannot be dated exactly but Cafone suggests in his bibliographjy that they were written between 1869–1874. The tracts were

published by the Willard Tract Repository, Boston and are available in the libraries of Oberlin College and Princeton Theological Seminary. They were reprinted in Charles Finney, *Power From on High*.

[88]Finney, *Power from on High*, p. 42.

[89]Ibid., pp. 39–40.

[90]Wright, pp. 267, 304.

[91]A discussion of the origin of these articles and brief summary of their content is found in Warfield, pp. 134–35. The first article appeared in the New York *Independent* on Jan. 18, 1872. They were later published separately as tracts and together as a *Package Series of Little Books for Christians* by Willard Tract Repository, Boston, n.d. They also appeared as an appendix to some later editions of Asa Mahan's *The Baptism of the Holy Ghost*. They are reprinted, along with some other tracts by Finney, in *Power from on High*.

[92]Finney, *Power from on High*, p. 7.

[93]Ibid., p. 8.

[94]Ibid., p. 10.

[95]Ibid.

[96]Ibid., p. 18.

CHAPTER 3

[1]Wright, p. 204.

[2]Finney, *Professing Christians*, p. 358.

[3]Finney, *Power from on High*, p. 40.

[4]Finney, *Systematic Theology*, p. 29.

[5]Ibid., pp. 11, 19, 29, 598.

[6]Finney, *Professing Christians*, p. 342; *Promise of the Spirit*, p. 158; *Systematic Theology*, p. 168.

[7]Finney, *Systematic Theology*, pp. 168, 174–75.

[8]Ibid. p. 38.

[9]Ibid. p. 41.

[10]Finney, *Heart of Truth*, pp. 174–75; *Systematic Theology*, pp. 132ff, 141, 165, 181.

[11]Finney, *Systematic Theology*, pp. 38–41.

[12]Ibid., pp. 135ff.

[13]Ibid., pp. 143.

[14]Ibid., p. 629.

[15]Ibid., p. 374.

[16]Ibid., pp. 370ff.

[17]Ibid., pp. 520–21.

[18]Finney, *Promise of the Spirit*, p. 261.

[19]Finney, *Promise of the Spirit*, pp. 133ff; *Systematic Theology*, pp. 605–10.

[20]Finney, *Power from on High*, p. 39; *Promise of the Spirit*, p. 139; *Systematic Theology*, p. 610.

[21]Finney, *Promise of the Spirit*, pp. 135, 144ff, 160; *Systematic Theology*, pp. 605–6, 691.

[22]Finney, *Promise of the Spirit*, p. 135.

[23]Finney, *Systematic Theology*, pp. 619ff.

[24]Wright, pp. 210, 248–49; Finney, *Professing Christians*, p. 464; Finney,

Systematic Theology, pp. 619, 721ff.

[25]Finney, Systematic Theology, pp. 617–619.

[26]Finney, Professing Christians, p. 346; Promise of the Spirit, pp. 172, 189; Systematic Theology, p. 715.

[27]Finney, Systematic Theology, p. 595.

[28]Ibid., p. 410.

[29]Ibid., pp. 409–10.

[30]Ibid., p. 413.

[31]Ibid., p. 414.

[32]Ibid.

[33]Finney, Promise of the Spirit, p. 78.

[34]Finney, Systematic Theology, p. 557.

[35]Ibid., pp. 595–96, my emphasis.

[36]"Finney's Letters No. 38," O.E. 3 (Sept. 29, 1841): 156.

[37]Finney, Systematic Theology, pp. 27, 35, 182.

[38]Ibid., p. 636.

[39]Ibid.

[40]Ibid., pp. 636–637.

[41]Ibid., p. 639.

[42]Ibid., p. 640.

[43]Ibid., pp. 637–84.

[44]Ibid., p. 658.

[45]Ibid., p. 644.

[46]Ibid., pp. 640, 647.

[47]Ibid., p. 649.

[48]Ibid., pp. 640, 642, 645, 469.

[49]Ibid., p. 655.

[50]Ibid., pp. 682–83.

[51]Ibid., p. 520.

[52]Ibid., p. 648.

[53]Finney, Power from on High, pp. 40–41.

[54]Finney, Sytematic Theology, pp. 643ff, 683–84.

[55]Warfield, pp. 90–95, 173–76.

[56]Cafone, pp. 195-96.

[57]Finney, Systematic Theology, pp. 630ff, 645, 649; Power from on High, pp. 59ff.

CHAPTER 4

[1]Finney, Power from on High, pp. 7–8; Promise of the Spirit, p. 263.

[2]Finney, Power from on High, p. 8.

[3]Finney, "How to Prevail With God," O.E. 13 (July 16, 1851): 113–15; Sermons on the Way of Salvation, p. 372; Revivals of Religion, p. 73.

[4]"Sermon Preached at the Ordination of Fourteen Young Men," O.E. 4 (Sept. 28, 1842): 153–157; Autobiography pp. 55–56; Power from on High, pp. 5, 20, 42; Promise of the Spirit, pp. 263–65.

[5]Finney, Power from on High, p. 9.

[6]Ibid., p. 10.

[7]James Gilchrist Lawson, Deeper Experiences of Famous Christians (Anderson,

In.: Warner Press, 1911), p. 175.

[8]Finney, Systematic Theology, pp. 405–8.

[9]Ibid., pp. 410–412.

[10]Finney, Revivals of Religion, pp. 8–12; Sermons on Important Subjects, pp. 20–21.

[11]Finney, Systematic Theology, p. 427.

[12]"Necessity and Nature of Divine Teaching," O.E. 5 (June 21, 1843): 17–19.

[13]Finney, Revivals of Religion, pp. 8–9.

[14]Finney, Sermons on Important Subjects, p. 33.

[15]Ibid., p. 35.

[16]Finney, Sermons on Gospel Themes, p. 248.

[17]Finney, Systematic Theology, pp. 414–26; "Necessity and Nature of Divine Teaching," O.E. 5 (June 21, 1843): 17–19.

[18]Finney, Systematic Theology, pp. 426–27.

[19]Ibid., pp. 508, 510–11.

[20]Ibid., pp. 643–44, 683–84.

[21]Ibid., pp. 426–27.

[22]Ibid. See also Autobiography, p. 155.

[23]Finney, Power from on High, pp. 44, 46, 55; Systematic Theology, p. 426.

[24]Finney, Power from on High, p. 9.

[25]Finney, "Ordination Sermon," O.E. 5 (Sept. 28, 1842): 153; Power from on High, p. 42; Sermons on Gospel Themes, p. 332.

[26]Finney, Power from on High, pp. 5, 17, 7, 20, 23.

[27]Finney, Autobiography, p. 95.

[28]Ibid., pp. 95, 97.

[29]Ibid., p. 44.

[30]Ibid., p. 97.

[31]Ibid.

[32]Finney, Revivals of Religion, p. 128.

[33]Finney, "Communion with God, Part 2," O.E. 2 (Sept. 9, 1840): 145.

[34]Finney, "Communion with God," O.E. 2 (Aug. 26, 1840): 137.

[35]Finney, Sermons on Gospel Themes, p. 323.

[36]Finney, Sermons on the Way of Salvation, p. 430.

[37]Finney, Sermons on Gospel Themes, p. 323.

[38]Finney, Revivals of Religion, p. 128.

[39]Ibid., pp. 93ff.

[40]Ibid., pp. 94ff.

[41]Ibid., p. 101.

[42]Finney, "How to Prevail with God," p. 114.

[43]Finney, Autobiography, pp. 36–37.

[44]Finney, Revivals of Religion, p. 70.

[45]Ibid., p. 65.

[46]Finney, Promise of the Spirit, p. 223.

[47]Finney, Sermons on the Way of Salvation, pp. 395–96.

[48]Ibid., pp. 398–99.

[49]Finney, "How to Prevail with God," p. 114.

[50]Finney, Sermons on the Way of Salvation, pp. 372ff.

[51]Finney, Revivals of Religion, p. 105.

[52]Finney, Revivals of Religion, pp. 102–3, 105; Reflections on Revivals, p. 65.

[53]Finney, Power from on High, pp. 7, 8.

[54]Finney, *Autobiography*, p. 378.

[55]Finney, *Sermons on Gospel Themes*, p. 409.

[56]Finney, *Sermons on the Way of Salvation*, p. 430.

[57]Ibid., p. 444.

[58]John Calvin, *Calvin's Institutes of the Christian Religion*, III:1.

[59]Finney, *Power from on High*, p. 24; *Systematic Theology*, p. 655.

[60]Finney, *Systematic Theology*, p. 666.

[61]Finney, *Power from on High*, p. 71.

[62]Finney, *Sermons on the Way of Salvation*, p. 442.

[63]Finney, *Systematic Theology*, p. 637.

[64]Cafone, p. 196.

[65]Finney, "Communion with God," p. 138.

CHAPTER 5

[1]Frederick D. Bruner, A *Theology of the Holy Spirit* (Grand Rapids: Eerdmans, 1970); James D. G. Dunn, *Baptism in the Holy Spirit* (London: S.C.M. Press, 1970).

[2]Finney, *Power from on High*, pp. 7, 16–17.

[3]Ibid., p. 18.

[4]Finney, "Ordination Sermon," p. 153.

[5]Finney, *Power from on High*, p. 18.

[6]Ibid., p. 7.

[7]Finney, *Promise of the Spirit*, p. 150.

[8]Ibid., pp. 148–49.

[9]Ibid., p. 160.

[10]Ibid., pp. 162, 190.

[11]Ibid., p. 187.

[12]Ibid., p. 190.

[13]Ibid., pp. 162, 190.

[14]Finney, *Professing Christians*, pp. 370–71, 387; *Sermons on Gospel Themes*, pp. 398ff; *Systematic Theology*, p. 679.

[15]Finney's interpretation is based on the Authorized (King James) Version which translates *pisteusantes* as an antecedent rather than a coincident aorist participle. The New International Version, on the other hand, translates the participle as coincident. Other translations, such as the New American Standard Bible, are ambiguous, allowing for either interpretation.

Examples of commentators who are in agreement with the King James rendering are Markus Barth, *Ephesians* Anchor Bible; (Garden City, N.Y.: Doubleday, 1974), p. 95; S. D. F. Salmond, "The Epistle to the Ephesians," *The Expositor's Greek Testament*, ed. Robertson Nicholl (Grand Rapids: Eerdmans, 1979 [reprint]), 2:266–67.

The interpretation of the New International Version is supported by E. K. Simpson, *Commentary on the Epistle to the Ephesians*, ed., F. F. Bruce (N.I.C., Grand Rapids: Eerdmans, 1957), p. 35.

For a discussion of the conflicting interpretations of this verse and similar passages in Acts (11:17, 19:2), see J. R. Williams, *The Gift of the Holy Spirit Today*, (Plainfield, N.J.: Logos, 1980) pp. 78, 81, 82.

[16]For Example, Howard M. Ervin, *These Are Not Drunken As Ye Suppose* Plainfield, N.J.: Logos, 1968), pp. 16–33.

[17]Finney, *The Promise of the Spirit*, p. 134.

[18]Clark Pinnock, *An Evangelical Theology of the Charismatic Renewal* (Madison, Wisconsin: Theological Students Fellowship Reprints, 1975).

[19]Dunn, p. 225.

[20]Ibid., pp. 55ff, 224ff.

[21]Bruner, p. 261.

[22]F. F. Bruce, *Epistle to the Ephesians* (London: Pickering and Inglis, 1961), p. 79 quoted in *The Laymans Commentary on the Holy Spirit*, revised, ed. John Rea (Plainfield, N.J.: Logos, 1974), p. 186.

[23]J. R. Williams, "Pentecostal Theology: A Neo-Pentecostal Viewpoint," in *Perspectives on the New Pentecostalism*, ed. R. P. Spittler (Grand Rapids: Baker, 1976), p. 82.

Similarly, Wesleyan writer Lawrence Wood argues for the view of "a single complex event of salvation" in which there are "two distinct but coordinate moments of conversion and Spirit Baptism" which are "genuinely continuous but temporally distinct," in *Pentecostal Grace* (Wilmore, Ky.: Asbury Publishing Co., 1980), pp. 264–65.

[24]Finney, *Power from on High*, pp. 39–40; *Promise of the Spirit*, p. 262.

CHAPTER 6

[1]Bruner, p. 115.

[2]Finney, *Sermons on the Way of Salvation*, p. 430.

[3]Finney, *Revivals of Religion*, pp. 122–23.

[4]Finney, *Sermons on the Way of Salvation*, p. 441.

[5]Finney, *Power from on High*, pp. 6, 17–18.

[6]See the illustration of this principle in Finney's *Autobiography*, pp. 139–49.

[7]Finney, *Sermons on the Way of Salvation*, p. 439.

[8]Finney, *Autobiography*, p. 112; also found in *Revivals of Religion*, pp. 103-4.

[9]Finney, *Sermons on the Way of Salvation*, pp. 439–40.

[10]Finney, *Power from on High*, p. 7.

[11]Finney, "Death to Sin," *O.E.* 2 (July 15, 1840): 114.

[12]Finney, *Revivals of Religion*, p. 134.

[13]Finney, *Power from on High*, pp. 6, 17–18; *Revivals of Religion*, p. 105.

[14]Finney, "Death to Sin," p. 113.

[15]Finney, *Power from on High*, pp. 26ff; *Way of Salvation*, pp. 372ff.

[16]Finney, *Power from on High*, pp. 26–27.

[17]Finney, *Sermons on the Way of Salvation*, pp. 401–2.

[18]Finney, *Revivals on Religion*, p. 137; *Way of Salvation*, p. 418.

[19]Finney, *Promise of the Spirit*, p. 191.

[20]Finney, *Power from on High*, pp. 60–61, 79ff; *Systematic Theology*, p. 629.

[21]Finney, *Systematic Theology*, p. 631.

[22]Finney, *Promise of the Spirit*, p. 189; *Systematic Theology*, p. 632.

[23]Finney, *Power from on High*, p. 70.

[24]Ibid., p. 63.

[25]Finney, *Systematic Theology*, pp. 533, 537.

[26]Finney, *Promise of the Spirit*, p. 188.

[27]Williams, *Gift of the Holy Spirit*, pp. 105–7.

[28]Ibid., p. 107.

[29]Ibid., p. 121.

[30]Bruner, pp. 250–51; Warfield, pp. 567, 610.

[31]Williams, *Gift of the Holy Spirit*, pp. 76–77.

[32]Finney, *Power from on High*, pp. 70–71.

[33]Finney, *Systematic Theology*, p. 645.

[34]Finney, *Sermons on Gospel Themes*, pp. 405–9.

[35]Bruner, p. 344.

[36]Ibid. p. 234.

[37]Ibid.

[38]Finney, *Promise of the Spirit*, p. 262.

[39]Finney, *Power from on High*, pp. 17–18; *Systematic Theology*, pp. 413, 637.

[40]Finney, "The Poor In Spirit," *O.E.*. 6 (Dec. 4, 1844): 193.

CHAPTER 7

[1]Smith, Preface to *Promise of the Spirit*, p. 3.

[2]Dayton, "Christian Perfection," pp. 41ff.

[3]Herbert McGonigle, "Pneumatological Nomenclature in Early Methodism," *Wesleyan Theological Journal* 8 (Spring, 1973): 61–72, referred to by Dayton, p. 41.

[4]Leo George Cox, *John Wesley's Concept of Perfection* (Kansas City: Beacon Hill Press, 1964), p. 132.

[5]Ibid., quoting Wesley's *Works* XII, 416, VI, 10–11.

[6]Ibid.

[7]Dayton, "Character Perfection," p. 42.

[8]Ibid., pp. 45–48.

[9]Ibid., pp. 43–47.

[10]Smith, "Introduction," p. 25, referring to George Peck, "Christian Perfection," *Methodist Quarterly Review* 22 (Jan. 1841): 128–32, 151–52.

[11]H. Orton Wiley and Paul T. Culbertson, *Introduction to Christian Theology* (Kansas City: Beacon Hill Press, 1946), pp. 302–3.

[12]Smith, *Revivalism and Social Reform*, pp. 103ff, 141.

[13]J. H. Fairchild, "The Doctrine of Sanctification of Oberlin" *Congregational Quarterly* 8 (April 1876): 237.

[14]Finney, "Salvation Always Conditional," *O.E.* 2 (Dec. 16, 1840): 202.

[15]Finney, "Sanctification, No. 1," *O.E.* 2 (Jan. 1, 1840).

[16]Hills, p. 226.

[17]Finney, *Autobiography*, p. 340; *Professing Christians*, pp. 358–59.

[18]Hills, p. 221.

[19]Ibid., p. 222.

[20]Finney, *Systematic Theology*, pp. 636–37.

[21]Ibid., pp. 370–72, 593.

[22]Hills, p. 226.

[23]Finney, "Prayer for a Pure Heart," *O.E.* 11 (March 14, 1849): p. 41.

[24]Ibid.

[25]Hills, p. 224.

[26]Finney, *Sermons on the Way of Salvation*, p. 443.

[27]Ibid., pp. 441–51.

[28]Steven Barabas, *So Great Salvation: The History and Message of the Keswick*

102 CHARLES G. FINNEY

Convention (Westwood, N.J.: Revell, 1952), pp. 21, 24.

29Smith, "Introduction," pp. 25–26.

30Barabas, pp. 43, 47–49.

31Ibid., pp. 1311–12.

32Ibid., p. 180.

33Ibid., p. 134.

34Ibid., p. 103.

35Ibid., p. 94.

36Ibid., p. 95.

37Evan H. Hopkins, quoted by Barabas, pp. 48–49.

38Finney, *Systematic Theology*, p. 650.

39Barabas, p. 94.

40Ibid., pp. 89, 93.

41Ibid., p. 94.

42Finney, *Sermons on Gospel Themes*, pp. 380–81.

43See George Eldon Ladd, A *Theology of the New Testament* (Grand Rapids: Eerdmans, 1974), pp. 485–86.

44Barabas, pp. 47–50.

45Ibid., p. 99.

46Ibid.

47Ladd, p. 524.

48Ibid., pp. 128-29.

49Stanley N. Gundry, *Love Them In: The Proclamation Theology of D. L. Moody* (Chicago: Moody Press, 1976), pp. 77–78.

50V. Raymond Edman, *They Found the Secret* (Grand Rapids: Zondervan, 1960), pp. 83–4; R. A. Torrey, *Why God Used D. L. Moody* (New York: Fleming H., Revell, 1923), pp. 51–54.

51Moody, quoted in Edman, *The Secret*, p. 85.

52Gundry, p. 153.

53Ibid.

54Torrey, *Why?* p. 51.

55Ibid., pp. 55ff.

56 Roger Martin, R. A. *Torrey: Apostle of Certainty* (Murfreesboro, Ind.: Sword of the Lord Publishers, 1976), pp. 72–73.

57R. A. Torrey, *The Baptism with the Holy Spirit* (New York: Fleming H. Revell, 1895); *The Holy Spirit: Who He Is and What He Does* (New York: Revell, 1927); *The Person and Work of the Holy Spirit* (New York, Revell, 1910); *What the Bible Teaches* (New York: Revell, 1898).

58Torrey, *The Baptism with the Holy Spirit*, p. 10.

59Ibid., pp. 14–15.

60Ibid., p. 16.

61Torrey, *The Person and Work of the Holy Spirit*, pp. 116ff.

62Ibid., pp. 182–83.

63Martin, p. 51.

64Finney, *Autobiography*, p. 55.

65*Baptism with the Holy Spirit*, pp. 22, 57–58; *The Holy Spirit: Who He Is and What He Does*, pp. 124, 196.

66*Baptism with the Holy Spirit*, p. 64.

67Bruner, p. 40.

[68]Ibid., p. 41.

[69]This summary of the history of Pentecostalism is based on the following: Melvin Dieter, "Wesleyan-Holiness Aspects of Pentecostal Origins" and William Menzies "The Non-Wesleyan Origins of the Pentecostal Movement" in *Aspects of Pentecostal-Charismatic Origins*, ed. Vinson Synan (Plainfield, N.J.: Logos, 1975); Vinson Synan, *The Holiness-Pentecostal Movement in the United States* (Grand Rapids: Eerdmans, 1971); Edith Waldvogel (now Blumhofer), "The Overcoming Life: A Study in the Reformed Evangelical Contribution to Pentecostalism," *Pneuma* (Spring, 1979): 7–19.

[70]Such as the Fire-baptized Holiness Church, Pentecostal Holiness Church, Church of God in Christ, and Church of God, Cleveland, Tenn.

[71]*Statement of Fundamental Truths*, Assemblies of God, U.S.A., paragraphs 6-7.

[72]Peter Hocken, "Jesus Christ and the Gifts of the Spirit," *Pneuma* 5 (Spring, 1983): 1–16.

[73]Smith Wigglesworth, quoted by Stanley H. Frodsham in *Smith Wigglesworth: Apostle of Faith* (Springfield, Mo.: Gospel Publishing House, 1948), p. 44.

[74]*Victory* (April, 1909) p. 1, quoted by Hocken, p. 4.

[75]*The Apostolic Faith* I (Sept. 1907), p. 3., quoted by Hocken, p. 5.

[76]*The Apostolic Faith* II (May 1908), p. 2, quoted by Hocken, p. 5.

[77]Hocken, p. 8.

[78]Ibid.

[79]Finney, *Systematic Theology*, p. 637.

[80]Finney, *Autobiography*, p. 20.

[81]Finney, *Promise of the Spirit*, p. 263.

[82]Henry Cowles, "The Baptism of the Holy Ghost," O.E. 2 (May 20, 1840): 86–87.

[83]Finney, "Death to Sin," O.E. 2 (July 15, 1840): 114.

[84]Finney, *Revivals of Religion*, p. 95.

[85]Ibid., p. 101.

[86]Finney, *Autobiography*, pp. 36-37.

[87]Finney, *Sermons on Gospel Themes*, p. 255.

[88]Finney, *Revivals of Religion*, p. 94ff.

[89]Ibid., p. 70.

[90]Finney, *Systematic Theology*, p. 636.

[91]Morton Kelsey, *Tongue Speaking* (New York: Doubleday, 1964), p. 221.

[92]Ibid., p. 231.

[93]Ibid., p. 227.

[94]Ibid., p. 232.

[95]Kelsey, *Encounter with God: A Theology of Christian Experience* (Minneapolis: Bethany Fellowship, 1972).

[96]Ibid., p. 165.

CHAPTER 8

[1]Hodge, p. 241; Warfield, p. 193.

[2]Cox, pp. 168ff.

[3]Finney, *Professing Christians*, p. 393.

[4]Cox, pp. 168ff.

[5]Paul Tillich, *Systematic Theology*, 3 vols. (Chicago: University of Chicago Press, 1951–63), 2:36-39.

SELECTED BIBLIOGRAPHY

Ahlstrom, Sidney E. *A Religious History of the American People*. New Haven: Yale University Press, 1972.

Barabas, Steven. *So Great Salvation: The History and Message of the Keswick Convention*. Westwood, N.J.: Revell, 1952.

Bruner, Frederick Dale. *A Theology of the Holy Spirit*. Grand Rapids: Eerdmans, 1970.

Cafone, James Michael. *The Role of the Holy Spirit in the Theology of Charles Finney*. Ph.D. dissertation, Catholic University of America, 1979.

Cox, Leo George. *John Wesley's Concept of Perfection*. Kansas City: Beacon Hill Press, 1964.

Day, Richard E. *Man of Like Passions: A Dramatic Biography of Charles G. Finney*. Grand Rapids: Zondervan, 1942.

Dayton, Donald. *Discovering an Evangelical Heritage*. New York: Harper and Row, 1976.

_____. "The Doctrine of the Baptism of the Holy Spirit: Its Emergence and Significance." *Wesleyan Theological Journal* 13 (Spring 1978): 114–124.

_____. "Theological Roots of Pentecostalism." *Pneuma: Journal of the Society for Pentecostal Studies* (Spring, 1980): 3–21.

Dunn, James D. G. *Baptism in the Holy Spirit*. London: S.C.M. Press, 1970.

Edman, V. Raymond. *Finney Lives On*. Minneapolis: Bethany Fellowship, 1951, reprinted 1971.

_____. *They Found the Secret*. Grand Rapids: Zondervan, 1960.

Ervin, Howard M. *These Are Not Drunken, As Ye Suppose*. Plainfield, New Jersey: Logos, 1968.

Fairchild, J. H. "The Doctrine of Sanctification at Oberlin." *Congregational Quarterly* 8 (April, 1876): 237–259.

Finney, Charles G. *Charles G. Finney: An Autobiography*. New York: Fleming H. Revell, 1908.

_____. *The Heart of Truth*. Minneapolis: Bethany Fellowship, 1976. (Originally titled *Skeletons of a Course of Theological Lectures*, 1840.).

_____. *Lectures on Systematic Theology*. London: William Tegg, 1851.

_____. *Lectures to Professing Christians*. New York: Fleming H. Revell, 1878.

_____. *Lectures on Revivals of Religion*. New York: Fleming H. Revell, 1868.

_____. *Power From on High*. Fort Washington, Penn.: Christian Literature Crusade, n.d.

_____. *The Promise of the Spirit*. Edited by Timothy L. Smith. Minneapolis: Bethany Fellowship, 1980.

_____. *Reflections on Revival*. Compiled by Donald Dayton. Minneapolis: Bethany Fellowship, 1979.

_____. *Sermons on Gospel Themes*. Manchester: James Robinson, n.d.

_____. *Sermons on Important Subjects*. New York: John S. Taylor, 1836.

_____. *Sermons on the Way of Salvation*. Oberlin, Ohio: E. J. Goodrich, 1891.

Foster, Frank H. *A Genetic History of the New England Theology*. Chicago: University of Chicago Press, 1907.

Frodsham, Stanley H. *Smith Wigglesworth: Apostle of Faith*. Springfield, Mo.: Gospel Publishing House, 1948.

Gundry, Stanley N. *Love Them In: The Proclamation Theology of D. L. Moody*. Chicago: Moody Press, 1976.

Haroutunian, Joseph. *Piety vs. Moralism: The Passing of the New England Theology*. New York: Henry Holt and Co., 1932.

Hills, A. M. *Life of Charles G. Finney*. Cincinnati: M. W. Knapp, 1902.

Hocken, Peter. "Jesus Christ and the Gifts of the Spirit." *Pneuma: Journal of the Society for Pentecostal Studies* 5 (Spring, 1983): 1–16.

Hodge, Charles. "Review of Finney's Systematic Theology." *Biblical Repertory and Princeton Review* 19 (1847): 237–277.

Holland, DeWitte, ed. *Preaching in American History*. Nashville: Abingdon Press, 1969.

Johnson, J. E. "Charles Finney and Oberlin Perfectionism." *Journal of Presbyterian History* 46 (1968): 42–57, 128–38.

_____. "Charles Finney and a Theology of Revivalism." *Church History* 38 (1969): 338–58.

Kelsey, Morton. *Encounter with God: A Theology of Christian Experience*. Minneapolis: Bethany Fellowship, 1972.

_____. *Tongue Speaking*. New York: Doubleday, 1964.

Lawson, James Gilchrist. *Deeper Experiences of Famous Christians*. Anderson, Ind.: The Warner Press, 1911.

McLoughlin, William G., Jr. *Modern Revivalism: Charles Grandison Finney to Billy Graham*. New York: The Ronald Press, 1959.

Mahan, Asa. *The Baptism of the Holy Ghost*. West Summerfield, B. C., Canada: The Friend of the Homeless Publishing House of Pure Religious Literature at Mizpah Heights, 1932.

Marsden, George M. *The Evangelical Mind and the New School Presbyterian Experience*. New Haven: Yale University Press, 1970.

Martin, Ralph. *R. A. Torrey: Apostle of Certainty*. Murfreesboro, Tenn.: Sword of the Lord Publishers, 1976.

The Oberlin Evangelist. Oberlin, Ohio, 1839–1862

Rea, John, ed. *The Layman's Commentary on the Holy Spirit*. Revised. Plainfield, New Jersey: Logos, 1974.

Scharpff, Paulus. *History of Evangelism*. Translated by Helga Bender. Grand Rapids: Eerdmans, 1966.

Smith, Timothy L. "The Doctrine of the Sanctifying Spirit: Finney's Synthesis of Wesleyan and Covenant Theology." *Wesleyan Theological Journal* 13 (Spring 1978): 92–113.

_____. *Revivalism and Social Reform in Mid-Nineteenth Century America*. Nashville: Abingdon Press, 1957.

————. "Righteousness and Hope: Christian Holiness and the Millennial Vision in America, 1800–1900." *The American Quarterly* 31 (Spring 1979): 21–45.

————. "Righteousness and Hope: How Finney Helped Americans Discover the New Covenant: Righteousness Through Grace." Introduction to *The Promise of the Spirit* by Charles G. Finney. Minneapolis: Bethany Fellowship, 1980.

Spittler, Russell P., ed. *Perspectives on the New Pentecostalism.* Grand Rapids: Baker Book House, 1976.

Statement of Fundamental Truths. General Council of the Assemblies of God, U.S.A. Springfield, Mo.: Gospel Publishing House.

Synan, Vinson, ed. *Aspects of Pentecostal Charismatic Origins.* Plainfield, New Jersey: Logos, 1975.

————. *The Holiness-Pentecostal Movement in the United States.* Grand Rapids: Eerdmans, 1971.

Torrey, R. A. *The Baptism with the Holy Spirit.* New York: Fleming H. Revell, 1895.

————. *The Holy Spirit: Who He Is and What He Does.* New York: Fleming H. Revell, 1927.

————. *The Person and Work of the Holy Spirit.* New York: Fleming H. Revell, 1910.

————. *What the Bible Teaches.* New York: Fleming H. Revell, 1898.

————. *Why God Used D. L. Moody.* New York: Fleming H. Revell, 1923.

Waldvogel (Blumhofer), Edith L. "The Overcoming Life: A Study in the Reformed Evangelical Contribution to Pentecostalism." *Pneuma: Journal of the Society for Pentecostal Studies* (Spring, 1979): 7–9.

Warfield, B. B. *Perfectionism.* 2 vols. New York: Oxford University Press, 1931.

Wiley, H. Orton, and Culbertson, Paul T. *Introduction to Christian Theology.* Kansas City: Beacon Hill Press, 1946.

Williams, J. Rodman. *The Gift of the Holy Spirit Today.* Plainfield, New Jersey: Logos, 1980.

Wood, Lawrence W. *Pentecostal Grace.* Wilmore, Kentucky: Francis Asbury Publishing Co., 1980.

Wright, G. Frederick. *Charles Grandison Finney.* New York: Houghton Mifflin and Co., 1891.

————. "Dr. Hodge's Misrepresentations of Pres. Finney's System of Teaching." *Bibliotheca Sacra* 33 (April 1876): 381–392.